THE SHEIK

Without anyone to guide him, the portrayal of the savage desert chieftain became almost entirely Rudolph's invention. He instilled within the role all of the powerful male characteristics he had learned to dam up within himself since his days as a gigolo. If his depiction was an overstatement, it was an overstatement that the newly emancipated women of the nation would thrive on. Women were to find in *The Sheik* a symbol of the omnipotent male who could dominate them as the men in their own lives could not. And the eventual success of the film was to sky-rocket the one-time bit part villain into screen immortality as the Great Lover.

VALENTINO
by Vincent Tajiri

VALENTINO

Vincent Tajiri

BANTAM BOOKS • LONDON
TORONTO • NEW YORK

VALENTINO

A Bantam Book / June 1977

ISBN 0-553-11098-5

Published simultaneously in the United States and Canada

Bantam Books are published by Bantam Books, Inc. Its trade-
mark, consisting of the words "Bantam Books" and the por-
trayal of a bantam, is registered in the United States Patent
Office and in other countries. Marca Registrada. Bantam
Books, Inc., 666 Fifth Avenue, New York, New York 10019.

PRINTED IN THE UNITED STATES OF AMERICA

ACKNOWLEDGMENTS

The author wishes to express grateful appreciation to: Charles Bloch, who originated and encouraged this work; Bev Chamberlain Janis, for her invaluable research assistance; the Academy of Motion Picture Arts and Sciences (Stills Library), Eddie Brandt, British National Film Archives (Stills Library), Culver Pictures, Larry Edmunds, The Museum of Modern Art, Susan Terry, Gene Trindle (Globe Photos), Universal Photographers, and United Press International, for providing many of the photographs; and Rose, Brion and Rea for their aid and understanding.

CONTENTS

PART ONE

PART TWO

PART THREE

PART ONE

"A part of your country remains with you forever. Even if more external signs are never visible. I look Italian, of course. But I have more characteristics of Italy than that. I don't relish cold weather. I am born in a tropical climate. For generations hot suns and fierce suns have penetrated the blood of my forefathers and it has come down to me, still alien to the cold."

—Rudolph Valentino
(from his diary)

AUGUST 23, 1976

It is a little past eleven in the morning and the mid-August sun burns bright and hot. The sky is typical of Los Angeles at this time of year: cloudless and blue, marred only occasionally by white streaks of jet trails. The limousine that turns off of Santa Monica Boulevard into the asphalt drive next to the huge sign that reads: HOLLYWOOD MEMORIAL PARK, is long and black and noiseless. A short distance inside the park it turns left onto a wide graveled pathway where it moves slowly, trailing a low cloud of dust, past people walking in the same direction who stare through its windows at the occupants. When it reaches the squared-off stone building with Doric columns that is the Cathedral Mausoleum, it glides to a stop. A uniformed chauffeur alights and hurries around the car to open the door for his passengers.

This is the twenty-third day of August, 1976—a day of deep significance to thousands the world over. On this date at 12:10 p.m., fifty years ago, Rudolph Valentino, the most beloved of all screen lovers, died in a hospital in New York. Each year since then, the faithful have gathered here at his burial site to mourn his passing.

There is something about all of this that borders on the implausible. Two generations have come since that era when the image of the noble shiek danced, romanced and cavorted on the screen and still a thousand people of all ages will come to mourn on this day. Is it not fair to assume that of those that will be here, a good proportion have never seen the movies of Valentino? The lure can be neither the man nor the screen

3

image—but the legend that has grown since his untimely death and continued to grow despite the fact that his movies are seldom shown. A legend that all who come only serve to perpetuate.

Intensely introspective, Valentino found the immensity of his popularity to be bewildering. This explanation he once summarized, "It is not what I am but what they think I am." With that single line he had touched upon the manner by which deities are created.

The limousine door is opened and from the oversized opening a small woman emerges. She is dressed entirely in black, a veil cloaks her features and dark sunglasses hide her eyes. She is old and infirm and is supported on her left side by a brawny man dressed in a dark suit. She leans on a cane as she walks—slowly, almost painfully. The oddly matched couple move past the main corridor lined with statuary to the inner hall where—in a sheltered alcove next to the arch of a stained glass window depicting a pastoral scene—the crypt awaits. It is faced by white marble with a bronze plaque—now darkened by the patina of years —on which the raised letters read: RODOLFO GUGLIELMI VALENTINO, 1895–1926.

She places a basket of flowers at the foot of the crypt and kneels as in silent prayer for several minutes. Rising, she blows a farewell kiss at the crypt, and moving slowly is gone. Across the basket of flowers a bright red ribbon holds the silver-metallic letters: POLA.

Those who have witnessed this brief episode whisper excitedly: Was it really Pola Negri, last of Valentino's loves, or was it merely a surrogate? No one really seems to know. There are even some within the crowd that insist that the mysterious woman in mourning drapes was actually Jean Acker, Valentino's first wife.

As the lighting of the torch symbolically opens the beginning of each Olympic games, the appearance of a Lady in Black has ritualistically marked the beginning of these memorials in honor of Rudolph Valentino. Within minutes the mourners have jammed themselves within the corridors of the mausoleum. Without adequate movement of air, the heat soon becomes stifling. Adding to the discomfort are the portable television lights aimed into the alcove where Jon Hall, the one-time movie hero of "island" epics, delivers a eulogy in which he credits Valentino as an inspiration to his career. Pressed into a corner of this alcove, the French actress Corinne Calvet—born the year of Valentino's death—holds smoldering sticks of incense as her eyes glisten. Seated within this tiny area is Mary MacLaren, white-haired and withered. A former silent screen actress, she, among all notables present, is probably the only one who has known the Great Lover personally. She speaks very softly, a frail little lady probing into her memories. "He once asked to take me dancing at the Alexandria Hotel—you know, the big one downtown—but my mother said I was too young."

How awful, a woman sighs, to have been asked to dance with Valentino and be told that you're too young.

The ceremonies end and the crowd pushes its way, with unhurried politeness, toward the exit where the sun is bright and the air—at 85 degrees—is considerably cooler. It is a grab-bag of people representing all age groups from tiny tots to senior citizens. Their attire exemplifies the non-uniformity that characterizes southern California dress—from chic to sloppy; neckties and suits to T-shirts and jeans; from polyester print dresses to elegant pants suits. Within the crowd are two men dressed in the robes of a Bedouin sheik and several women dressed in the style of the Casbah.

With the alcove now cleared, a thin, sharp-featured man with thinning hair—gray at the temples and slicked back—takes over the position in front of the Valentino crypt. He carries an undeniable air of authority. "Yes," he says, in answer to a question, "the Lady in Black was Pola. Poor girl. As you know, she's practically penniless now. Heaven knows how she managed to scrape up the sixty dollars it cost her for the limousine."

One of the women asks if she may have a flower from Pola's bouquet as a memento. The sharp-featured man obliges by removing a white carnation from the basket and graciously hands it to her. Apparently swept away by the maganimity of this gesture, he now proceeds to remove a handful of flowers which he begins to pass to any who will take one. At this point

there is a loud shout, "What are you doing there?"
Two women push their way into the alcove and, after
identifying themselves as friends of the Valentino family, ask, "Who are you?" and without waiting for a
reply, "What right have you to give away these flowers. They're part of the memorial and are not to be given
away."

The thin man mutters, "I've been instructed to
give flowers to some of the older women." He turns
quickly and disappears down the corridor.

One of the recipients of flowers, a smallish woman in
a hat of woven straw, moves quickly over to Pola's
basket and replaces a flower. "See," she announces, "I
put mine back." But no one is paying attention.

Outside, a large man with thick-lensed glasses beck-
ons toward a group standing on the stairs of the
mausoleum. "Come with us. We're all going over to
Delongpre Park. We've got the statue up again."

The reference is to a bronze sculpture—an Egyp-
tian-like male nude with its head tilted heavenwards
—created in the memory of Valentino in 1930. Titled
"Aspirations," it is the work of Roger Noble Burnham.
Shortly after being installed in the park, it became the
target of vandals. One night it was torn from its base
to be found a few days later in an alley several blocks
away—completely defaced by paint. For safekeep-
ing, it had been stored until now in a warehouse; but
on the occasion of this fiftieth anniversary of Valentino's death, it has been restored to its original place
in the park.

The last of the crowd now moves along the gravel
drive toward their cars. For those familiar with the
life of the most famous of all screen lovers, the site is
not without its subtle ironies. A few yards west of the
mausoleum, the ground dips sharply down to a long,
rectangular reflecting pool at the end of which is a
magnificent shrine—the Napoleonic tomb of Douglas
Fairbanks, Sr. If there was one actor whom Valentino
envied—one person whom he most wanted to emulate
—it was the dashing, athletic Fairbanks, whose acting
talents were equaled only by his business acumen.
Valentino's remains lie next to those of June Math-

is, the screenwriter who discovered him and from whom his crypt was first borrowed before being purchased. Fairbanks rests in a plot that runs almost the length of the mausoleum, and his tomb stands alone in the open —out in the sunlight.

Behind the mausoleum, less than a hundred yards to the south, the Memorial Park ends abruptly where corrugated gray-metal sidings wall the rear boundary of Paramount Studios. In the early twenties, when Paramount ruled the industry under Adolph Zukor and Jesse Lasky, Valentino was its foremost male star. Then, when his career was at its height, came his courageous battle against the studio for control over his films—a fight that would cost him a year's suspension from filmmaking.

Northward the weathered tombstones jut out un-evenly over patches of browning grass. The trees that surround appear aged and weary. The cars are leaving. They move into Santa Monica Boulevard where, to the west, the street is lined with titillation for sale—massage parlors, nude wrestling, adult book stores and porno theaters. To the east, Western Avenue is much the same. Directly ahead the Pierce Brothers Mortuary corners a street on which are rows of stucco houses in fading pinks, yellows and whites. A short distance beyond, the ground rises to meet the hills that shelter this once-fabled land. A land that once held a magic as illusionary as the lives that passed through it. Its name is inscribed along the hills in giant white letters that catch the bright sunlight: HOLLYWOOD.

GENESIS

Shortly before midnight, *donna* Gabriella awoke to wetness and the involuntary tightening of her abdominal muscles. Calmly, she aroused her husband and told him that the time had come. He awoke, muttering. Body awkward with sleep, he felt his way to the dresser where he found the candles and lighted them. Pulling his trousers over his nightshirt, he rushed to the house of his brother to solicit the assistance of his sister-in-law and her mother, who had been awaiting such a call for the past week. By the time he returned to his home, he was fully awake and after a brief conversation with his wife—whispered, so as to not awaken their two young children—he moved into the practiced ritual of making preparations for the delivery of his third child.

Giovanni Guglielmi was skilled at such matters and he was rightfully proud of his abilities. As the highly respected practitioner of veterinary sciences for Castellaneta—and the area that surrounded that tiny village twenty miles from the southernmost tip of Italy—he had delivered hundreds of kids, calves and colts over the years and, when emergency warranted, had brought many a baby squalling into the world.

Gabriella's period of labor was short. The delivery clean and simple. Some time after the new infant had been bathed, wrapped and bedded in the cradle that stood at the foot of the bed, Giovanni moved away from the small group of clucking women and went alone into the back room that served as his study and office. Here by the flickering light of candles, he made an entry into the family log: "May 6, 1895. 3 a.m.

9

Birth of our third child. A son . . ." He stopped, his forehead creased with thought. Instinctively, he reached for one of the pipes he kept on his desk. Filling it with tobacco from a jar, he lit it and leaning back in his chair took several deep drags—meditating. Then, exchanging his pipe for the pen, he added: ". . . named, Rodolfo."

Here he sat for uncounted moments, his eyes directed—unseeing—at the open journal. He inhaled deeply from his pipe and the warm tobacco smoke soothed the tensions within him. He felt the strange mixture of exhilaration and gnawing anxieties. The third child had brought both joy and additional responsibilities. To Giovanni, life had been a constant opponent.

His musings were broken by his brother who entered the room with a glass of wine, and he agreed to join the others, embracing each of them again as they toasted the newborn. After they had left he went to the room where his older children slept and, looking down on their placid faces, whispered, "Beatrice, Alberto. You now have a baby brother."

He then returned to his wife's bedside. Exhausted from the ordeal she was in deep sleep. Holding her hand, he knelt by the bed and, though not a profoundly religious man, he offered his thanks to the Mother Mary, the Christ child, and the Holy Father. Dawn found him sitting on a chair by the bed, his thoughts filled with concern. Thus far he had bested life in the continuing struggle, but his trips into tiny villages and the remote areas had brought him face to face with those who had succumbed. The *Mediogiorno,* the southern part of Italy, was the dry well of abject poverty. A state of existence that the people referred to as *la miseria,* a word of Latin derivation that in the English language became misery.

During the years that followed, the people of southern Italy would seek escape from *la miseria* by emigrating, in increasing numbers, to other lands. One land that would receive the majority of these emigrants would be that which had been founded on hope. A new land named after an early Italian explorer—America. By

1905, Italians would make up half of the total of new emigrants entering the United States and this would grow until the rate exceeded 200,000 Italian emigrants annually.

As sunlight filled the room where Giovanni Guglielmi sat, his newborn son stirred quietly in his cradle. Through eyes still unused to sight he gazed in wonderment at the play of shadows and light across the ceiling. At that moment, in that very land of hope, the play of light and shadow was the obsessive concern of others, men who had spent years studying ways of capturing the movement of life on film. Their efforts were finally coming to fruition and would one day result in projecting the newly born infant into the consciousness of people the world over.

He was a child filled with paradoxes. Adults, strangers and young girls found him shy, reserved and often uncommunicative. Yet, when at play with the boys in the neighborhood he was bold, gregarious and the leader when it came to dangerous escapades. These contradictions find easy explanations. Adults were his superiors and young girls imbued with a mystical angelic quality and he was reverent in their presence. His peers looked much like him, so among them he was completely natural.

Less explainable was the combination of gentleness and wildness that lay within him. The gentleness would always be a part of him, while as he grew older, the wildness would become restrained, coming forth in the form of rebellion.

Gabriella, with a fault common to mothers, would at first see only the appealing gentleness in her son and this touched her greatly. When the mothers of other boys came to complain about Rodolfo's fighting, or his enticing their sons to join him in some mischievous escapade, she was quick to defend him until, eventually, the evidence and incidents became impossible to deny. Then, she would scold her son passionately, but after the fury had been spent she would find herself tearfully embracing the child. As he grew older and bigger she began calling on Giovanni to punish him, and the father would reach for the riding crop that hung in his workroom. It was a task that his father had little stomach for, and the need of it angered him and often added to the force of his blows.

Rodolfo's first encounter with death came with the passing of his older sister, Beatrice, when he was five. Though he could not fully comprehend its meaning, he was disturbed by the totality of his parents' bereavement. The realization that Beatrice would never be around again to take his hand and tease or scold him came slowly. When his father died, he was eleven. By then he understood the permanency of death, and the tragedy tore into him. There had been a shared closeness between the father and his second son—one that was seldom spoken or overtly demonstrated. There were times when their eyes had met and smiles emerged, times when hair was fondly rumpled and laughter shared. But that was the extent of it. In the years to come Rodolfo would gradually realize that Giovanni Guglielmi was less than the fearsome giant who had towered over him. That he may not have been the bravest and strongest of all cavalry officers during his military career. That he had been merely a man like other men—a bit more serious or stolid but not much different. And it would be only then, in his adulthood, that Rodolfo would begin to know his father.

Shortly after his father's death, the family moved to Taranto, a larger seaport city that lay in the arch of Italy's boot. It was but twenty kilometers from Castellaneta but, for the children, it might have been another planet. Having only known the quietude and the unhurried indolence of a small rural village, they had problems adjusting to smaller quarters and the bustle of a larger city. The rebellion within Rodolfo became more apparent, and he fell into a pattern of running away on trips that would take him back to the rocky hills of Castellaneta where he would find solace within the caves he knew so well.

His disappearance would bring panic to his family and relatives, who would imagine the worst. And upon his return—unharmed, contrite and famished—he would first be embraced tearfully and then his uncle would administer punishment.

Among the neighbors he became known as incorrigible, a reputation that, though not completely warranted, served to divorce him from the company of the nicer boys in his new environs. Gabriella, frustrated by her inability to cope with one who was without malice but troublesome, nevertheless, came to a decision that was approved at a gathering of her relatives. In order to learn discipline, she sent him off to military school.

Rodolfo was not prepared for the strictly regimented life of the military school. He was constantly punished, deprived of privileges and considered the class dunce. On the occasion of King Vittorio Emmanuele's visit to the town where the school was located, Rodolfo had been stripped of his clothing and confined to quarters. This failed to stop him. After the others had left to join the parade, Rodolfo broke into the room where the uniforms were kept, found one that most closely approximated his size, although much too large, took a sword and, with the horses all gone, found a donkey he could ride and joined the parade. The following day he was expelled and returned to Gabriella.

They tried sending him to a naval academy for youngsters and he was rejected because his chest measurements, when expanded, fell below the minimum requirements. Gabriella was not without a solution. "Italy needs scientific farmers more than they need soldiers or sailors," she told her distraught son, and she entered him in the Royal Agricultural Academy outside of Genoa.

This time he was determined to succeed and he did well. While not a brilliant student, he was quick to learn and soon found himself popular with his classmates. When he returned home a graduate, he walked straight and tall and exuded an air of confidence. Yet after a couple of weeks, the old restlessness seemed to be coming back to him. He had been away from home too long to easily fit back into the routine. He took to wandering about alone. He went back to Castellaneta where he found little in common with those whom he had known.

He had discovered, while in school, that he had an intuitive facility for languages and had become fluent in French. He left again. This time, Gabriella noticed that some of the money she had put aside for him was missing. When he returned, several weeks later, he said he had been to Paris. As for the money, it had all been spent but would be paid back, and he now knew what he wanted to do. On his travels he had met people who were bound for America. They were in need of laborers and money was plentiful. "I'll soon pay you back and when I return I'll buy a villa on a hill. A lovely villa such as you've seen up north."

The argument that followed went into the night and began again the next day. Finally, frustrated by her inability to change her son's mind, Gabriella called her relatives together for assistance.

It was a typical family council gathering. It began with warm embraces, kisses and laughter. Eventually the men gathered at one end of the room with the women at the other. At first the room resounded with laughter and talk. And then the purpose of the meeting was presented and the room grew quiet. Questions were asked. Answers were given and more questions came forth. Decorum gave way and heated arguments arose and dissipated. All of the women sided with Gabriella: certainly there was work available in Taranto—even for someone as proud as Rodolfo. And, if not in Taranto, surely in Napoli or Roma where at least he could come home easily on occasion.

The men seemed divided. Some sided with their wives, others argued against them. Finally, an older cousin whose success had earned him both respect and authority stood and, gesturing, asked for quiet. "Let him go," he announced. "It will do him good to have to fight for his very existence in a country where he knows neither the customs nor the language. It will either make a man of him or it will break him. Here he will be ruined because his heart is not in it. And if he is to become a criminal as some say he is destined, then let it be in America where he will not bring disgrace upon all us here."

"Let the wastrel go," said an uncle who had previously argued against Rodolfo leaving. And so it was that the decision was reached. Women gathered around Gabriella—weeping and shaking their fists at Rodolfo. And the men poured wine and drank to Rodolfo's health. It was agreed that all would contribute money so that he would have something to live on until he found a suitable job.

All told, the sum to be given Rodolfo as a farewell send-off would amount to four thousand lira. (In later years Rodolfo would claim the stake had been four thousand dollars—a highly unlikely figure for the historically poverty-stricken south of Italy.) In early December 1913, Rodolfo Guglielmi, surrendering to tearful embraces, left Taranto for New York City where on December 23, he would find himself emerging from the subterranean caverns of Grand Central Station where he had come by subway after having cleared Ellis Island. A suitcase in one hand, a cloth bag tossed over his shoulder, he would search the faces of passersby, stopping those who looked Italian, so that he could produce the paper in his pocket that bore the address of the apartment house on West 49th Street named Giolitto's and have the way pointed out for him.

Only in Paris had he seen such large buildings. But these were taller and there were endless rows of them. He eventually found 49th Street, crossed Fifth Avenue, bedecked with Christmas trimmings, and headed west toward Broadway.

A SOCIETY SENSATION

There are times and places where one can be completely isolated and still not be lonely. There are other times and places where one can be among a million people or more and be painfully lonely. Hustling, bustling New York City during the Christmas and New Year's holidays can be—to the friendless—the loneliest place in the universe. The deep canyons between tall buildings and the festive, milling crowds amplify one's insignificance. There is the sound of music and laughter that is not for you; cafés filled with people who belong to each other and none to whom you belong. For an immigrant—foreign to the language and customs—there can be no worse time to be in New York City.

At Giolitto's he had made an immediate impression on the landlady. Initially shown a tiny room—third floor rear, where he would have to share the bathroom down the hall with four others—he shook his head and politely asked if there wasn't anything larger. He was shown, and took, the best available, a two-room suite, with a private bathroom, on the street side. He paid in advance and left the landlady wondering whether her new tenant was a scion of wealth or a fool.

After inspecting the closets, playing with the water taps, and marveling at the manner in which the toilet flushed when he pulled the chain that hung from the water box on the ceiling, he sat by the tall windows and watched the traffic as it moved down 49th Street. Never had he seen so many motorcars together before. Counting them as they moved past, he found that they outnumbered the horse-drawn wagons. After the newness of this had lessened, he unpacked his bags, took his pocketknife, cut a few threads of stitching, and removed several bills of large denominations from the linings of his coat. Counting his monetary assets and computing the rate of exchange, he figured that he had approximately $750. At a time when the average American family income was around $20 per week, he was very well off.

Rodolfo's early days in New York were filled with new experiences. It was the nights that were difficult. He spent the days in exploration and, though he often felt a need to communicate with someone, his fascination with the strange new sights and sounds dispelled loneliness. He rode the streetcars and the subways and he walked over much of midtown Manhattan. He bought newspapers that he learned to read with the aid of his Italian-English dictionary, and he ate in cafeterias where he could select food by sight rather than by words.

It was in the late evenings that the loneliness welled inside rose to confront him. He found some solace in writing letters describing everything from the modern plumbing to the strange custom of the people who chewed a substance called "gum." He even bought packages of this unusual product with the name that was impossible to pronounce, Wrigley's, sending one to Italy and keeping the others to chew—which he did with flaunting nonchalance, whenever he felt observed.

It was a restaurant called Bustanoby's and a personable waiter named Henri that were to change the pattern of his lonely existence. Passing by the restaurant he noticed that the menu in the window listed its bill of fare mostly in French. Once seated inside he was delighted when the waiter greeted him in French, and he responded in kind. He felt an instant camaraderie with this man who, he learned, was named Henri. Soon it became a nightly custom for him to dine at Bustanoby's and, after a while, he would automatically be shown to a table at Henri's station. On nights when business was slow, Henri would stop by his table for extended conversations and would, occasionally, bring over a special *patisserie* at the end of dinner —compliments of the house.

Catering to a European clientele, styled in the look of a French restaurant, a friendly ambiance prevailed at Bustanoby's. For once, Rodolfo felt that he belonged. He began to recognize the regulars and was recognized by them. Customarily, there would be greetings upon arrival and waves at departures. One evening, three men who periodically would occupy a table adjacent to Rodolfo's, invited him to join them. Overjoyed, Rodolfo moved over to the fourth, unoccupied chair at their table.

The three men introduced themselves as George Ragni, from France, and two brothers from Austria, Count Alex and Count Otto Salm. That evening, Rodolfo joined his newfound friends on a tour of nightclubs. It was the most enjoyable evening that Rodolfo had known since arriving in New York and, during the course of it, he found himself dancing with a girl who began to teach him the "new steps that are the rage"—the one-step and the tango.

During the weeks that followed, it became a Friday night custom for the foursome to meet at dinner prior to going out to clubs where they would dance until the early hours of the morning. Rodolfo was quick to master the rhythm and movements of the tango and soon, as the most expert dancer of the group, he was, as an inside joke, being introduced as "Count" Rodolfo di Valentina.

The name and title had come about from a discourse on family histories. Rodolfo had mentioned the belief that his family were descendents of royalty and that his full name was: Rodolfo Alfonzo Raffaelo Pierre Filibert Guglielmi di Valentina d'Antonguolla. Following that recitation, he had said laughingly, "You know how we Italians are. No matter how poor we may be, we are always rich in names."

Nothing, it is commonly said, lasts forever, and money least of all. By the spring of 1914, Rodolfo found that the high style of living he had been enjoying had considerably lowered his funds. Growing desperate, he

went to the offices of the commissioner of immigration
and found, when listing his job qualifications, that there
was little to say beyond indicating that he had graduated from the Royal Academy of Agriculture in Santa
Ilario Ligure, a tiny village outside of Genoa. His tim-
ing was fortunate. The millionaire Cornelius Bliss, Jr.,
was looking for a qualified gardener who could convert
the landscaping at his Long Island estate into a repre-
sentation of an Italian garden.

After a brief interview, Rodolfo was hired for room,
board and a small salary. While he lacked a work
history in the U.S. and looked quite young, his new
employer was impressed by the papers that indicated
that Rodolfo had graduated from the Royal Academy
of Agriculture. He had no way of knowing that the
school with that impressive title had a curriculum
equivalent to a trade school at the high school level in
America.

It had been a long, cold winter and the earth was
still frozen and hard. There was little for the new
Italian gardener to do but walk about the estate making
sketches of the changes he would propose. One day he
observed a motorcycle that another worker at the estate had parked beside a shed. He straddled it, bent
over the bars and imagined himself roaring down a
road, "Brrroooom!" There was no one around. What
would it hurt, he thought, if I just took it for a little
spin? He kicked down on the starter, throttled it, and
rode up to the top of a hill. There he lit a cigarette,
feeling excited and good. Below the hill several girls
were walking along talking. One pointed up at him.
Another waved. Impulsively, Rodolfo started the engine again and, this time lying horizontally with his
stomach on the seat, he drove down the hill toward
them. The speed—accelerated by the incline—was
more than he could handle and the machine went out
of control, careening into a telephone pole. Thrown
clear, he found himself uninjured but the fender of the
motorcycle was badly damaged.

Rodolfo made his apologies to the owner of the
two-wheeled machine and agreed to pay for all repairs.
"You see," he explained, "I am crazy about machines.

They hypnotize me and I cannot resist them." A few days following the incident, Bliss called him in to inform him that, regretfully, his wife had decided that she no longer wanted to have an Italian garden. Instead, she was thinking about a small golf course. Therefore, his services were no longer required.

He returned to the commissioner of immigration and was sent to an estate in New Jersey. Here he discovered that the position was not as a landscape architect as he had expected, but strictly one involving manual labor, a job he considered beneath his dignity. He quit after two weeks and was paid seven dollars and fifty cents above his room and board.

He came to rue his pride. The immigration people informed him that in America, despite whatever myth he may have heard, no one started at the top. He moved to a boardinghouse and from there to smaller lodgings—each one more confined, more shabby than the one preceding. He took odd jobs, washing dishes, polishing brass, sweeping up stores. He ate at Horn and Hardart's automat which he learned to call the "Hungry and Homeless." He would stop at a tavern to avail himself of the free lunches. At the last rooming house, where he was evicted for non-payment of rent, the landlady retained his luggage. New York was not as easily conquered as he had originally believed.

Still, he clung to his pride, tin-plated though it may have been. He would stop in at the Astor Hotel and filch stationery to write optimistic letters on the expensive paper with the hotel's crest: "Things are a little slow right now because of the summer season, but there are some very big things coming up in the fall and I'll soon be sending you money."

When he could no longer afford the price of a bed, he found himself spending the night in Central Park. After three nights in the park, he met a fellow Italian who was in similar circumstances. The difference was that his newfound friend had a room he was willing to share. Also, he had some straight advice: "Look, it doesn't matter how well you've been educated or how fine your family is. You say you're humble. Well, you have to be more humble. You say you are willing to work at anything. Well, go out and beg for work if necessary."

The next day he went to Maxim's, an elegant mid-town café, to see if they needed kitchen help. While there he saw a familiar face. It was Henri, the waiter from Bustanoby's who had become the headwaiter at Maxim's. Henri remembered him. "I've got an idea," he said. "You were a good dancer, weren't you? Do you want to dance?"

"Surely. But what kind of dancing?"

Henri explained. The new dance craze, the tango, had brought interest in social dancing to a fever pitch, and to keep up with competing cabarets, Maxim's had inaugurated the afternoon *thé dansant*. More and more unescorted women—in pairs and in groups—came to the cabarets during the late afternoon hours, where they would sip tea or champagne while they munched on dainty finger sandwiches, gosisp, and dance. To meet an obvious need, Maxim's had begun to hire attractive men who were excellent dancers to serve as instructors and dance partners. The basic salary was minimal but the women had been found to be generous with their tips.

To be paid for dancing with attractive women, Rodolfo thought, must be akin to bribing a child to eat candy. He borrowed enough money to get his dress suit out of pawn and bathed, shaved and utterly immaculate, he showed up that evening.

There was something very special about this sleek man with the narrowed, intense look and pantherlike grace. His polished manner—borrowed from studying the Salms'—was decidedly continental, as was his amusing, convoluted English spoken with a decided accent. He was flirtatiously aggressive, constantly intimating sex but never to the extent of intimidating. He introduced himself as Rodolfo di Valentina and the rumors suggested that he was of a titled family and had been forced to flee from the war in Europe, leaving all his funds behind. Soon his income from tips—supplemented with monies received from private lessons—grew abundantly. In addition there were little favors given him: silk scarves, handkerchiefs, cuff links, neckties and, from one enamored admirer, a gold cigarette case with his initials boldly inscribed. It was not long before he was being asked by women whose husbands were out of town—or occupied in other affairs—to escort them to private parties among the smart café society set.

At one of these parties he met one of Flo Ziegfeld's newest stars, a perky little blond named Mae Murray. Mae, who had previously been a dancer at the Sans Souci, was featured in Zeigfeld's "Merry Pickums" number, a satiric takeoff on the rising darling of the movies, Mary Pickford.

What brought them together was the knowledge that they shared. Neither really belonged, nor would they ever be totally accepted, in the society in which they found themselves. Their tenuous membership was based neither on family wealth nor social status but on the ephemeral whims of others. Beyond that, there was a similarity of backgrounds. Mae's father, Rodolfo learned, had also died while she was very young. While he had been sent off to private schools, she had been placed in a convent. At the age of thirteen, she ran away from the convent, leaving behind her real name: Marie Adrienne Koenig, an identity that Mae Murray would forever deny.

It was a relationship that both sorely needed at the time. Each was living a life of artifice. Regarded as sexual objects, they were in need of a close, platonic relationship, very natural and very neuter.

While Rodolfo had to fend off the amorous advances of occasional partners to survive, Mae's problems were concentrated in two men who pursued her avidly: Jack De Saulles, who was married, and Jay O'Brien, who was not. To complicate matters further, the two were friends and the battle for Mae's affections had become a matter of personal egos. While, to Mae, Rodolfo represented a calm port that harbored her from a turbulent sea, to her two admirers he was inexplicable competition.

When Jay O'Brien confronted Mae about spending a considerable amount of her time with "that Italian gigolo," Mae thrust out her chin defiantly. "You don't have to worry about Rudy," she said. "Nothing ever happens with him. He might as well be a priest."

Jay was in love with her. With Jack it seemed to be strictly a compulsive need to conquer. Jay was insanely jealous, and the times she spent with him were tempestuous and emotionally draining. He wanted marriage and she was not prepared for any sort of binding commitment. Jack was married to a lovely South American girl, Bianca, a situation that he had no intention of changing. Jack could be handled. He merely wanted to bed her.

On their evenings together, Mae and Rodolfo would occasionally join Jack and Bianca. Completely disregarding his wife's presence, Jack would immediately address his attention toward Mae. The first time this occurred, Rodolfo, sensing Bianca's embarrassment, asked her to dance. To flatter her ego, he turned on his practiced charms. As she began to respond, he suddenly realized how lovely a woman she was. Soon he fell in love with Bianca De Saulles. She was a striking beauty with pale, unblemished skin and large dark eyes that sparkled when she was happy. Her father was one of the most prominent men in Chile and her mother was recognized as one of the most beautiful of its women. Bianca's beauty was said to rival that of her mother's. To Rodolfo, Bianca had the look of a madonna. As their acquaintanceship grew, love blossomed. While her husband was involved with his various "business enterprises," Bianca began dropping by Maxim's.

His love for Bianca began to make Rodolfo discontented with his way of life. He observed that it was not only a sham but parasitic. He started to look about for other opportunities, and soon he found one. A friend introduced him to dancer Bonnie Glass whose partner, Clifton Webb, was leaving to try his hand at acting. Glass and Webb had been the top-billed dance act at theaters in the New York area, and now Bonnie Glass was in need of a new partner.

Roldolfo auditioned for her and was accepted at a salary of fifty dollars a week. To one accustomed to averaging easily twice that amount, it was a comedown, but the opportunity of escaping from a profession he was beginning to despise was worth the sacrifice. After a week's rehearsal the new team made its debut at a charity affair at Delmonico's, and then moved into a booking at the Winter Garden. This was followed by a tour of the Keith and Orpheum theaters; later, they played the Colonial and the famed Palace Theater. While Bonnie enjoyed life as a performer, the uncertainties of the business motivated her to invest in something that might still be around when her good looks and the spring in her legs began to depart. She took over the basement of the old Boulevard Cafe and opened a cabaret restaurant called the Montmartre. This provided a solid home base for the dance team between outside engagements.

One of Rodolfo's most memorable moments occurred during this time. A successful out-of-town tour took them into Washington, D.C., for a week's engagement. On opening night they heard an excited murmur run through the audience, followed by a standing ovation as President and Mrs. Woodrow Wilson made an entrance into a box adjacent to the stage. He would savor the memory for years to come. "Imagine," he would tell his friends, "this dumb, twenty-year-old wop performing before the President of the United States!"

That evening they had danced inspired. Rodolfo counted sixteen curtain calls.

In the summer of 1916, Bonnie Glass closed the Montmartre. By fall she was back in business with another cabaret, the Chez Fisher on West 55th Street. This second enterprise was also to be short-lived. Bonnie had found a type of security more meaningful to her— she married Ben Ali Haggin, a wealthy scenic designer.

Rodolfo was once again unemployed. But unemployment, this time around was not without its warm and tender moments.

He signed with the William Morris agency and made the rounds of audition calls for chorus boys in musicals. In his abundant free time, he began to see Bianca De Saulles. Bianca insisted they had nothing to hide. They dined at Rectors, Bustanoby's, the Ritz Grill, and

danced at the finest cabarets. It was not long before
Jack De Saulles became aware of his wife's activities
and it may be likely that this was Bianca's intent.

At this point, Joan Sawyer entered the picture.

Joan had been a one-time child star with Gus Edwards' "School Daze" vaudeville troupe of talented
youngsters, which would also graduate George Jessel,
Eddie Cantor and Walter Winchell. After leaving Edwards, she had established herself as a top-flight exhibi-
tion dancer. Hearing of Bonnie Glass' retirement, and in
need of a new partner, she contacted Rodolfo and
found him eager. He was hired and they went off into a
tour of the vaudeville houses.

Under New York state law at that time, the only
legally acceptable ground for divorce was adultery.
Rumors said that Rodolfo had pledged he would aid
Bianca in obtaining the divorce her husband denied
her. Someday, he had said, Jack De Saulles would be
incontestably caught in an adulterous act.

In July 1916, Bianca De Saulles filed suit against
her husband for divorce, an action based on adultery.
Named as corespondent was Joan Sawyer, dancer.
Among the witnesses who testified in behalf of the
plaintiff was Rodolfo Guglielmi. On September 15,
Bianca was granted her divorce.

A year later, Bianca was to assure the permanency
of her separation from Jack De Saulles. In an argument
over the possession of their child, Bianca shot her
philandering ex-husband.

During the interim between Bianca's divorce and
Jack's death, Rodolfo was having problems of his own.
The extent of his involvement in the De Saulles divorce
had many versions among the ranks of show business
people and few of these favored Rodolfo. If top jobs
were not easy to find before, they now became well
nigh impossible. Infrequently he would find a job in
the chorus of small musicals that soon died aborn-
ing. As far as the café society set was concerned, he
was completely ostracized. His welcome in New York
had worn thin.

The William Morris office informed him that a musical comedy troupe, *The Masked Model,* was planning a

cross-country tour that would take it to San Francisco, and there was an opening in the cast for a good male dancer. Rodolfo had heard that San Francisco possessed a scenic beauty much like parts of Italy. Many Italians had moved there to become fishermen, others had settled in the immediate environs where the climate was ideal for the growing of grapes. The soil held strength and security, something that could not be said for dancing. Bonnie Glass' words came to him, "When your looks are gone, your legs gone, then you'll soon be gone."

Something else suggested that he should leave New York City. Bianca De Saulles' trial for the shooting of her husband had been scheduled. Friends informed him that should he be subpoenaed, testimony might make a case for his deportation. If he wanted to stay in the U.S., San Francisco was about as far away as he could get.

He applied for the job and was hired. Unfortunately, *The Masked Model* had never been rated for distance. It folded in the stretch—Ogden, Utah, to be precise. Stage props, costumes and equipment were put up for sale and the proceeds divided among the actors and other personnel as payment for salaries due. The amount received by Rodolfo Guglielmi was barely enough to take him back to New York, or onward to San Francisco with change to spare. There were no second thoughts, he chose the latter.

There was a freshness about San Francisco. Rising out of the ashes of decimation by quake and fire in 1906, the city had rebuilt itself rapidly to host the Panama-Pacific Exposition in 1915.

The city by the bay welcomed the flow of transients from the east but rolled out no red carpets for those without money. Employment could be found, but for those with meager skills it was at the bottom of the labor market where requisites were limited to strong hands and a sturdy back. Rodolfo felt that he was destined for a better fate.

He looked up millionaire Jack Spreckels in his mansion atop Nob Hill, overlooking the bay, and told him of his desire to obtain a plot of land where he could raise grapes. Spreckels referred him to A. P. Giannini, president of the Bank of Italy, who informed the confident young man with illusions of immediate success that his lack of business experience made him a poor risk for a loan. The banker advised Rodolfo that—first things first—he should find a steady job and begin by saving some money toward his dream.

Rodolfo began looking for work and, after several lean weeks, found employment as an instructor in a rundown dance academy. Here in a loft, to the tunes of a player piano, he struggled with young housewives and office girls for a small salary and no tips. Within a few weeks, Rodolfo decided he had had enough. The final straw came about with an incident provoked by a sexually aggressive student whose sole interest seemed to be to arrange a meeting elsewhere to explore more satisfying activities. Insulted at being rejected, she spat in his face and stormed out. Rudolfo informed his employer that he would leave at the end of the week.

His next job was also of short duration. The touring company of a musical comedy, *Nobody Home,* hired him as a dancer during its three week engagement in San Francisco. Following that, he was again at liberty.

America's entry into the World War had brought forth a spate of recruitment posters urging able young men to enlist in the military. Finding himself drifting about without a job of any permanence, Rodolfo began to give more and more thought to a glorified career as a soldier. His father had been a military man, why not follow in the family tradition? One poster he found to be particularly appealing. It showed an enormous biplane swooping down from a red sky across which were the words: "Join the Air Service and Serve in France. Do It Now."

He tried to enlist in the Canadian Flying Corps and was rejected. He went to the Italian Consulate and was again turned down. Discouraged, he took a job as a salesman.

It was then that he heard that a movie crew was in San Francisco filming *The Little Princess* starring Mary Pickford. He dropped by the location to inquire into the possibilities of getting an acting job and ran into Norman Kaiser, an actor whom he had known from New York. They agreed to meet later in the bar at the Fairmont Hotel.

"It's not Norman Kaiser anymore, it's Norman Kerry," his old friend explained over drinks at the Fairmont. "Had to change it. The patriots here would lynch me with my real name."

Kerry had done exceptionally well since moving out to Los Angeles and was now playing starring roles. This one, in which he played opposite Pickford, was for her new studio, a division of Paramount called Artcraft. There was big money to be made in movies: Adolph Zukor, he said, was rumored to be paying Mary Pickford $10,000 a week plus a percentage of the box office receipts.

Rodolfo was intrigued: "Would there be work for me if I came down there?"

Kerry's response was optimistic. There was always a need for extras, and with his help he could get Rodolfo into bit parts. "Wait, I've got an idea. Frank Carter's in town and maybe I can arrange something." Carter, the husband of Broadway star Marilyn Miller, was the road manager for Al Jolson's *The Passing Show,* which would be moving from its performances in San Francisco to a booking in Los Angeles.

The next day Kerry informed Rodolfo that it had all been arranged. Carter had agreed to hire him as a dancer and he could travel with the troupe to appear with them in Los Angeles.

"When you get into L.A., come over to the Alexandria. You can stay with me until you get settled," Kerry added.

EYES OF YOUTH

When Rodolfo entered the marble-columned lobby of the Alexandria Hotel, he began to sense that, for once, he had hooked the brass ring. As he walked across the "million-dollar" oriental rug that had known the tread of Paderewski, Caruso and Sarah Bernhardt, he felt the excitement growing within him. Later, during his first few days, he sat amongst screen heros like Douglas Fairbanks and William S. Hart in the bar of the Alexandria and was introduced to director Emmett Kelly, who offered him work in a film called *Alimony*.

Hired as an extra at the going rate of five dollars per day, Rodolfo found himself in a familiar setting in *Alimony*. Cast as a background player for a ballroom scene, he was attired in the "uniform" of Maxim's, a full-dress suit. The star of the film, Josephine Whittel, was the wife of the Broadway matinee idol, Robert Warwick. In minor roles were two young girls whose rapidly rising careers were to bring them together with Rodolfo in the future. One was a saucy brunette with large, impassioned eyes named Lois Wilson; she was less than two years away from becoming a leading lady. The other was a very attractive blond named Alice Taffe, who would later become a star as Alice Terry.

Rodolfo was hopeful that quick fame and wealth lay ahead. However, he was soon to learn that Hollywood took little interest in someone who looked foreign. The all-American-boy look was in. And unless an actor looked like Wallace Reid, Charles Ray, Jack Pickford or Thomas Meighan, the roles were scarce and limited to more villainous parts—the "heavies."

The roots of the tenacity displayed by Rodolfo during these uncertain months were anchored in the knowledge that for once, in all his young years, he had found something that appealed to him more than anything else. He found an excitement in acting. Searching for a personal identity, he found temporary substance in placing himself into the role of a manufactured individual unflawed by his own doubts and weaknesses.

While he had vowed never to return to dancing, circumstances forced him back. He found work at the Watts Tavern, a roadhouse in the southern suburbs frequented by movie people. His partner was Margaret Tain who would later find success as a featured player with Christie Comedies. He was paid thirty-five dollars a week; enough to allow him to move into an apartment of his own a few blocks west of the Alexandria.

The move to new quarters did not keep him from spending most of his afternoons in and around the Gentlemen's Bar at the Alexandria. One day, while entering, he ran into Emmett Flynn who was just leaving. "Rudy," the director called out, "have you seen Hayden Talbot? He's been looking for you."

Flynn went on to explain that Talbot, who had written the scenario for *Alimony,* had been impressed by the poise and ease with which Rodolfo carried himself in evening clothes. He had now completed a scenario for a new film titled *The Married Virgin* in which the heavy was an Italian count, and had Rodolfo in mind when he wrote the part. The script had been purchased by a newcomer to films, a former New York music hall producer named Joseph Maxwell.

"Maxwell's staying here," Flynn said. "Why don't you give him a call and tell him that you're the fellow Hayden had in mind when he wrote the story."

Rodolfo met with Maxwell and after a short discussion won the role at a salary of fifty dollars a week.

Rodolfo's hopes that the success of the film would bring producers knocking at his door soon dissipated. Few in the industry or out bothered to see *The Married Virgin*. Having given up steady employment at the Watts Tavern, he was again scrounging around for work. Norman Kerry again came to the rescue. Starring in Emmett Kelly's film, *Virtuous Sinners,* Kerry asked the director if any work could be found in the picture for his friend. Kelly obliged by putting Rodolfo on the payroll at seven-fifty a day for the length of the shooting, despite the fact that his services were not needed for much of the time.

During his evenings at the Alexandria, Rodolfo learned that Mae Murray, who had become a star for Adolph Zukor in New York, had moved to Hollywood with her new love, director Robert Z. Leonard. They were filming over at the Universal City facilities. He decided to take a trip over to renew his acquaintance with Mae. While there, he was offered the role of a knight in *The Big Little Person.* Instructed to pick up a knight's armor at a costumer, he was given a tacky imitation of the real thing. He refused to accept the costume. He made a determined round of dealers in antique artifacts until he found an authentic suit of armor which, unlike the imitation, was solidly constructed out of metal and extremely heavy. The rental charge was fifteen dollars more per day than the imitation suit, a price he had to pay out of his own pocket when the production people refused to pick up the additional charge. When his scene was called, Rodolfo required the help of six property men to mount his horse. At this point the sun disappeared behind the clouds and the camera crew and cast had to wait until it reappeared. It was a warm day and the wait for the sun took three hours. All this time he sat on his horse, sweltering in the heavy suit. When the sun finally reappeared, the scene itself took only ten minutes to shoot. But it took several hours to extricate and revive Rodolfo.

Rodolfo's efforts in *The Big Little Person* impressed Leonard to the extent that he cast the young Italian as an Irishman, Jimmy Calhoun, in Mae's next picture *The Delicious Little Devil.* Somehow, the dedication and intensity that Rodolfo poured into his acting brought about a believable ethnic transition.

It did not escape Leonard's attention that Mae and Rodolfo had renewed the closeness they had shared in New York. On one occasion Mae, who kept a group of musicians on the set to aid her in playing a scene with the proper mood music, had the band strike up a tango while the company was between scenes. Leonard, who had been off the set on other matters, returned to find his girl friend dancing with Rodolfo. "This is a movie set, not a ballroom," he bellowed.

This film was the last for which Leonard hired the young Italian, but his respect for Rodolfo's talents resulted in a recommendation to Paul Powell, who was Carmel Myers' director. Powell used the film newcomer in two movies opposite Carmel Myers. For the first, *A Society Sensation,* Rodolfo was paid $125 a week; for the second, *All Night,* he was upped to $150.

Film production in Hollywood, which had begun to slacken noticeably during the summer of 1918, came to a virtual halt in the fall of the year. The cause was the worst influenza epidemic in the history of the nation. Theaters across the nation turned off the lights of the marquees and locked their doors. The studios suspended all shooting. Rodolfo decided to visit San Francisco to see friends. With his film credits, he hoped to find some work in the theater. What he found was the virus and he returned home to lay in bed fighting the illness. Believing that medical aid was a sign of weakness, he subsisted on boiled fruits and thick broths. When he recovered, he had lost thirty pounds.

On November 11, the Armistice was signed. While the news and the wild celebration that followed only held up production for a few days, theater owners eventually began to notice that war films were playing to empty seats. People wanted to put the war behind them, now that it was over. Many films based on war themes were canceled.

It was during this time that Rodolfo di Valentina moved closer to Anglicizing his name. He became Rudolpho Valentino, and soon the last "o" would be dropped from his first name. He also began to realize that, while he was moving into better-paying roles, his future seemed to be limited to secondary parts. The industry had typecast him as a heavy, a gigolo, or a titled foreigner. He began to put aside his dreams of stardom.

An old friend, Earle Williams, called him. Williams was starring in *A Rogue's Romance,* and they had a part for an apache dancer. Valentino hurried to the set, changed into costume, and danced for director James Young. "Son, where did you learn the apache?" asked the director.

Rudy smiled. "In Paris," he said.

"Well, you can't beat that for authenticity," Young replied and instructed his cameraman to stay on the dance scene for many more minutes than was originally intended. Although he was unaware of it, the extra footage he'd introduced would, in time, make his film much more valuable.

Young's final words to his apache dancer were, "Valentino, you've got a lot of ability. Work hard and you'll become a great actor."

Glowing from Young's comments, Rudolph went to work for Thomas Ince in *The Homebreaker,* a film starring Dorothy Dalton. He was cast as the villain. Much of Rudolph ended up on the cutting room floor. The extent of Rudolph's time on the screen in the released version was limited to one scene, running under a minute. Life seemed to be filled with ups and downs.

A call from D. W. Griffith's office offering him a part in Dorothy Gish's film *Out of Luck* sent his spirit soaring again. He had met the great director through a letter of introduction provided him by Paul Powell some time before. Upon leaving Griffith, he had felt disappointed. For much of the time, the hawk-faced director hadn't seemed to be paying attention to him. Now he felt good again—Griffith had remembered him.

Actually, it was Dorothy Gish who had instigated the call. Having seen his work, she felt that he would be ideal for the part of a gigolo. Griffith happened by the set while Rudolph was rehearsing a scene in which he was required to make amorous advances to a rich dowager in a café. Griffith commented favorably on Valentino's acting and then called director Elmer Clifton over.

"Elmer, this is the scene where the audience first meets the gigolo. You've got to establish the man's character immediately. Have the woman look away to watch the dancers. As she does this, the gigolo should hold her strand of pearls, study them, and then bite one to test whether it's real."

It was this type of inventive "business" that had made Griffith great and this lesson would not be lost on the young actor.

Shortly thereafter, Rudolph was introduced to the prestigious halls of the Los Angeles Athletic Club by Douglas Gerrard, an actor turned director who had become one of his better friends. While the Alexandria was the meeting place for those in the movie industry, the Athletic Club was where the elite of the city's social and business worlds met during the cocktail hour. It was here he first encountered several people who were to become friends and influence his future. One of these was Charles Chaplin.

Another was Pauline Fredericks, a highly-respected Broadway actress who had been lured to Hollywood by Adolph Zukor. Still another was Harry Reichenbach, probably the best known and most inventive of the industry's publicity men, who was also working for the Zukor-Lasky organization. Reichenbach took an immediate liking to the sleek young man with courtly mannerisms and suggested that he look up another friend of his, Herbert Sanford, manager of Clara Kimball Young. He had heard that Sanford was looking for someone like Valentino for a role in Young's next movie, *Eyes of Youth*.

The role offered by Sanford was similar to those that had been his fare since his arrival in Hollywood. Not only had Rudolph been typecast, but the characters he had to play all brought echoes from his past: dancers, gigolos and bogus counts. This one had an especially uncomfortable familiarity. It was the role of a professional corespondent, a man who earned his living by luring women into adulterous situations in which they would be trapped by divorce-seeking husbands.

Eyes of Youth was specifically aimed at the growing popularity of occultism. The heroine, played by Young, faces a situation requiring her to make one of three decisions regarding her future: 1) she can pursue her ambitions to become an opera singer; or give up her dreams for, 2) marriage to the man she loves, a struggling young engineer (Edmund Lowe) who must leave for South America; or, 3) save her father's business by marrying an older rich man (Milton Sills) whom she does not love. At the height of her dilemma, an Indian seer comes to visit, bringing with him a crystal ball that will give her a look into what will occur in each case.

Valentino's role was limited to the third episode. After marrying Young, Sills tires of his wife and decides to trap her in a compromising situation. Valentino is hired for the job and tricks Young into coming to his room on the pretense that her husband has been taken there after being seriously injured. The distraught wife rushes into the trap and Valentino, setting up evidence of a tryst, calmly pours drinks prior to his forced seduction attempt. As Young tries to fight off his embrace, the husband and a witness break into the room.

While Valentino played the role of the villainous seducer with lustful perfection, the reactions of the women in the audience were unexpected. Instead of finding him contemptible, the women were strangely stimulated by the arrogant competence of his polished seduction technique. Accustomed to seeing all-American males who blushed as they gave their girls a peck on the cheek—or heroic cowboys who preferred to nuzzle their horses, the appearance of an aggressive lover whose sole interest was forcing women into an act that would be mutually pleasurable opened the door to hidden fantasies. While the word would not get back to the moviemakers for some time, the vanguard of the newly liberated woman who would be shimmying, Charlestoning, black-bottoming and roaring into the twenties with a hip flask under her garter had arrived.

Only a few weeks after he had completed *Eyes of Youth,* the letter arrived. It was from Alberto, and Rudolph knew intuitively that it bore a grim message. He tore the envelope open quickly to learn that his mother had died. Grief and guilt overcame him. He read the letter over and over again, searching the words for nuances, until the wetness in his eyes would let him read no more.

He had not seen anyone for three days when Douglas Gerrard dropped by on a Sunday afternoon. Gerrard, quickly apprised of the situation and discovering that Rudolph had eaten but little over the past few days, insisted that they go out.

"C'mon," he said, "the worst thing is for you to sit around here feeling sorry for yourself. Your mother wouldn't have wanted you to turn into a monk or starve to death. Let's get some air, a drink and some food."

They drove out on Santa Monica Boulevard to the ocean where they walked along the sands and skipped rocks across the waters. Later, they had a quiet dinner and finished off a bottle of wine. On the way back, Gerrard turned into Sunset Boulevard and pulled into the semicircular drive in front of Pauline Fredericks' palatial home.

The Sunday afternoon-evening soirees of Pauline Fredericks had become a ritual for many in the new Hollywood society. Friends became accustomed to dropping by for drinks and a helping from the buffet prior to stepping out for the evening, or dropping by after dinner to dance to an orchestra playing "Ja Da," "Dardanella," "My Buddy" and other hits of the day.

Gerrard and Rudolph walked into a festive scene. Within moments after their arrival, the stately dark-haired hostess disengaged herself from a group with whom she had been chatting and, with long graceful strides, came over to them.

After welcoming them she walked them over to the bar, stopping every once in a while to see that they were introduced to other guests. One of the women to whom Rudolph was introduced appealed to him. He felt a pliant submissiveness in this brown-haired, petite beauty whose name was Jean Acker. At a time when his mind was filled with memories of his mother, he was attracted to similar qualities in this girl. They talked. She was under contract to Metro and had appeared in several movies, but her career had never taken off despite a promising start. As a seventeen-year-old she had made her debut in a starring role in *The Five-Million-Dollar Counterfeiting Plot,* playing opposite the real-life detective, William J. Burns. Her most recent movie had been *Checkers* with Thomas Carrigan, where she had secondary billing. Now she was acting in a minor role in a movie starring Alla Nazimova.

She said very quietly, "I was there at the Ship's Cafe when you came over to Nazimova's party. There was no reason for her rudeness and I told her so. It must have been terrible for you."

Rudolph flushed at the memory. It had been one of the most embarrassing moments in his life. The executives at Metro were giving Nazimova—the former Russian star of the Broadway stage whom they had brought to Hollywood—a party on the occasion of the completion of her film *Stranger Than Death*. Nazimova had been escorted by Charles Bryant, the wealthy financier, whom she often introduced as her husband. Even those close to Nazimova were not certain as to whether a marital state existed between the two, but knowing of the Russian actress' stable of young women "protégées," most believed that her relationship to Bryant was restricted to business and social convenience. At the party, Nazimova had insulted Valentino, calling him a gigolo and a pimp.

Noticing how uncomfortable Rudolph had become, Jean suggested that they dance and she was relieved to find that dancing relaxed him. Caught by the music, he was gracefully twirling her about the floor.

They began to see a lot of each other and each found that the other filled a need. How much was love and how much was an escape from loneliness is impossible to discern.

There was still occasional movie work. Rudolph had a small role in *An Adventuress,* which starred Julian Eltinge, the most famous female impersonator of the period. Aside from his ability to move and speak exactly like a woman, Eltinge had a collection of wigs and gowns that was the envy of all of the female stars. Another member of the cast was a vivacious brunette who had worked her way up from the Sennett comedies —a friendly, buxom girl named Virginia Rappe who was a year and a half away from her scandalous death in a San Francisco hotel. The aftermath would end the film career of a $5,000 a week comedian, Roscoe "Fatty" Arbuckle.

Another villainous role in Metro's *The Cheater* followed, undoubtedly a result of Jean's friendship with Max Karger, her studio boss. Jean's recommendation included the information that, since the part required that the heavy be dressed in full dress with white tie, her boyfriend would be ideal, since he owned several custom-tailored suits of that type.

Eyes of Youth opened at Tally's Kinema in Los Angeles on November 2, 1919, and the reviewers were strong in their raves about the unique story and the acting of Clara Kimball Young. One reviewer went on to praise "one of the most remarkable casts ever assembled for a picture." But Valentino was deeply disappointed; he was not mentioned in any of the reviews.

Three days after the opening of *Eyes of Youth,* Rudolph and Jean Acker were married, apparently on impulse. They had been horseback riding through Beverly Hills when Jean mentioned how romantic it was. Rudolph suggested that it would be even more romantic if they found a justice of the peace.

"You'd better not be serious about that because I may take you up on it," said Jean.

"I am serious," came the reply.

When they broke the news to Max Karger, he seemed overjoyed. "Dick will be going back into New York so I'm planning a small party for him at the Hollywood Hotel tomorrow night. Why don't the two of you get married at the hotel. We'll all have a big dinner and celebrate with the studio picking up the bill for everything."

Jean thought it was a great idea. "Dick," after all, was Richard Rowland, president of Metro. To be married and feted in his presence would be an honor. Rudolph was less certain but agreeable. He sensed that the industry in which he was a mere pawn was now invading his private life to use him.

After the wedding Jean drank much more than she should have. About two in the morning, Rudolph talked her into leaving the party to go to the honeymoon suite rented for them. As he gallantly opened the door and tried to carry her across the threshold, she refused to be picked up. In the short disagreement that followed, she pushed him aside, stepped into the room, slammed the door and locked it from inside. Thinking it was a bad joke, Rudolph pounded on the door. The only response was a tired "Go away! Leave me alone!" He continued to pound for twenty minutes, stopping only to beg her to open the door. There was no further response. She had either passed out or was no longer speaking to him. Chagrined, he gave up and went to his apartment to spend his wedding night alone.

Returning to the hotel in the morning, he tried knocking on the door of the room again. When there was no response he went down to the desk and asked for a duplicate key. He was informed that "Mrs. Valentino has checked out."

Utterly humiliated, he sought out friends for advice and consolation; Norman Kerry on one occasion, Doug Gerrard on another. They sympathized with him and suggested that it might have been the rush of events that had frightened Jean. "Give her time to think about it. If she loves you, she'll come back." He began hanging around the Metro lot, hoping to catch her. She was not around and no one knew where she might be staying. In desperation he went to see Max Karger. Karger admitted he knew where she was: "Around six o'clock in the morning, she came over to the house saying that she had checked out of the hotel. She was crying and asked if she could stay over. She said that she had made a terrible mistake and was sorry because she knew how you must feel. The next day she went to stay with a friend."

The friend was Grace Darmond. Bits of conversations clicked in Rudolph's mind. There had been several mentions by Jean about "her friend" and once or twice she had mentioned the name "Grace." Rudolph had never pressed her with questions. He only knew that the two had been very close before a quarrel had separated them just before he'd met Jean.

He learned that Grace Darmond was an actress who had starred in minor features made by Selig and Pathé.

She lived in an apartment in a building owned by her mother. He went to the house and knocked on the door. A woman's voice asked, "Who is it?" When he replied and asked for Jean, the voice said, "She's not here. She doesn't want to see you. Go away and leave her alone." When he asked that the door be opened so that he could talk, the woman's voice became insistent. "If you don't go away, I'll call the police." Rudolph left.

After persistent phone calls to the Darmond apartment, Jean finally agreed to speak with him. A few days later she agreed to meet with him. The meeting failed to resolve anything. She stated that she wasn't ready for marriage, that it had been a mistake. He took to writing letters. In one, dated November 22, 1919, he wrote, "Since I cannot force my presence upon you . . . I guess I better give up." But he had no intention of giving up, not just yet, for the letter went on, "I am always ready to furnish you a home and the comfort to the best of my moderate means and ability, as well as all the love and care of a husband . . . Please, dear Jean, darling, come to your senses and give me an opportunity to prove my sincere love and eternal devotion . . . Your unhappy husband, Rodolfo."

During this time of travail, the curly-haired Doug Gerrard—whose deep-set eyes were as brooding as Rudolph's—became Valentino's closest friend and constant companion. They would be seen dining or driving around town in Gerrard's runabout. While visiting the Metro lot one day, they ran into Jean. Stopping for a curbside meeting, they found her not only relaxed but quite friendly. She accepted Rudolph's invitation to visit his apartment, where they might start working out their problems, and Gerrard dropped them off there, feeling that a reconciliation was surely in the making. It was not to be. The following day Gerrard received a phone call from Rudolph. Jean had left him again.

In mid-December, Jean Acker went off on location to work on a film starring Fatty Arbuckle and Rudolph received a call from Norman Kerry. There was a role for him in a film Kerry was doing for First National. The film was called *Passion's Playground,* a light, romantic drama about life in the environs of Monte Carlo. Kerry had the starring role and Rudolph, in a small part, played his brother.

In answer to his daily letters, Jean wired Rudolph from the Arbuckle location: "I CANNOT PROMISE TO VISIT CHRISTMAS. HEARTBROKEN BUT WORK BEFORE PLEASURE. BE A GOOD BOY. REMEMBER ME EVERY SECOND. JEAN." However, whatever hope may have been awakened in Rudolph was soon to be ended. On January 11, 1920, the day after Jean Acker returned from location, there was an angry argument between the two at Jean's new apartment. This time, when Rudolph left, it was for good.

His first role after the break-up was as a villainous Italian count in Universal's *Once to Every Woman,* a melodrama in which he ends the career of an opera singer, Dorothy Phillips, by shooting her in the throat. But the specter of his love for Jean still haunted him. Reminders of her were everywhere in the city: the cafés they had frequented, the streets and parks they'd walked and even the bridle path along Sunset Boulevard. Doug Gerrard suggested that perhaps Rudolph should go to New York for a while. He gave Rudolph the names of directors and actors whom he knew, and other friends supplied additional names. In the early months of 1920, Rudolph returned to the city from which he had once fled.

The roles available to him in New York were no different from those he had done in Hollywood. His first movie for Pioneer was *Stolen Moments,* which starred Marguerite Namara and in which he played a romantic villain. Then came another role as a heavy for a Selznick film directed by George Archinbaud called *The Fog.* It was at this time that he noticed in *Variety* that Metro had purchased rights to Vicente Blasco Ibañez's best-selling novel *The Four Horsemen of the Apocalypse.* He paid little attention until a friend suggested that he would be ideal for the role of Julio Desnoyers, a secondary character in the story. After reading the book, Rudolph decided that his friend had been right—he was Julio. On a day when he wasn't required on the set he walked into Metro's New York office, identified himself and asked if he might see Richard Rowland.

The receptionist studied him carefully. Too many ambitious actors had tried to bluff their way into seeing the president of Metro on the pretense that they were "old friends."

"Mr. Rowland is in conference now," she said, "but I'll tell him you're here."

Rudolph took a chair and looked around him. The reception room was filled with posters of current Metro pictures: *Alias Jimmy Valentine* starring Bert Lytell. *Shore Acres* with Alice Lake and Frank Brownlee. And, there was Bonnie Glass' former dancing partner, Clifton Webb, who was featured in *Polly with a Past,* starring Ina Claire and Ralph Graves.

The girl returned. "Mr. Rowland will see you in a few minutes. He was curious how we found you so quickly," she said. With a touch of coyness, she added, "Tell me, how did we find you?"

The question bewildered Rudolph. "Tell him you just looked up and there I was," he said, smiling.

A buzzer sounded. "Mr. Rowland will see you now. It's the corner office."

Rowland met Valentino at the door. They shook hands and Rowland said, "We heard you were in town but didn't know where you were."

"I've been working with George Archinbaud over at Selznick."

"Well, that's one place we hadn't checked. What's the name of the project you're working in?"

"Well, until yesterday it was called *The Fog.* Now George tells me that they're planning to change the title to *The Wonderful Chance.*"

Rowland laughed. "That's a good move. Out of *The Fog* into *The Wonderful Chance.* The change should help it at the box office. Talking about wonderful chances, how'd you like to do a picture for us?"

"Well, if it's another Italian heavy, Dick . . ." he paused. He noticed that a rather short, slightly heavy woman with a dark cloche hat pulled over bobbed hair was sitting next to Rowland's big desk smiling at him. "Well . . . what I really wanted to talk to you about was *The Four Horsemen*." He couldn't pronounce the word "apocalypse" and would always avoid its use whenever reference to the film was necessary.

Rowland chuckled. "If that's what you came to see me about, you should speak to the lady over there. She made a special trip to New York to find you. Rudolph Valentino, meet June Mathis."

THE WONDERFUL CHANCE

In the microcosm called Hollywood—ruled by tough, shrewd men who had gambled, bargained and fought their way out of earlier careers as junk dealers, penny arcade operators, sellers of used clothing, June Mathis was a refreshing anomaly. Diminutive, decidedly feminine, she had come quickly out of obscurity to become the most powerful woman executive of the day.

Still, despite her success, this was not her goal. Given her choice, June Mathis might have forfeited her position as head of Metro's scenario department for the accolades that come to a famous actress.

The ambition that had once gripped her—and had been set aside some years back for the practicalities of a steady income, was born while she was still a young girl in Colorado. One evening she had been taken to see a traveling company of actors perform in a one-night stand at the town hall, and the magic of the theater had enraptured her. Later, when the family had moved to San Francisco, she found her way into drama groups and worked her way up until she was recognized for her sparkling performances in ingenue roles.

In 1914 she had come to Los Angeles as a member of the cast of *The Fascinating Widow,* which starred Julian Eltinge. When the show folded in Los Angeles after a few performances, June followed Eltinge and other members of the cast exploring the possibilities of acting roles in motion pictures. Infrequent bit parts convinced her that Hollywood was glutted with starry-eyed ingenues, most of whom were more attractive than she. June found a job writing scenarios.

Bright, possessed with boundless energy, and extremely articulate, June discovered that while the business end of the industry was an exclusive male society, the creative areas were receptive to the talents of women. Mary Pickford, Nazimova, Clara Kimball Young and Norma Talmadge were not only among the top moneymakers; they were, in actuality, independent producers affiliated with studios for the conveniences of having stages, lighting equipment, crews, wardrobes and the essentials of promotion and distribution available to them. With top actresses producing women-oriented films, there was a need for talented women on the story end. By the time she was 27, June Mathis was recognized as among the best of Metro's writers.

The project that had brought her to Richard Rowland's office had its beginning in 1918, when the translated version of Vicente Blasco Ibañez's *The Four Horsemen of the Apocalypse* first appeared in bookstores. It became an instantaneous best-seller. In mid-1919, when Richard Rowland was offered the screen rights to the book, he looked upon it as a gift horse. The paradox inherent within the situation baffled him. Here, at a time when movies about war were poison, was a war book that the public loved.

Of all of Metro's top executives, only June favored purchase of film rights. She explained the book's success: "It's not a war story—the theme is anti-war." Rowland found himself in full agreement. He countered the asking price of thirty thousand with an offer of twenty thousand, plus ten percent of the profits. Ibañez accepted and June was put in charge of the film.

Curious about life and its mysteries, June was fascinated by the occult. This interest had taken her to seances, spiritualists, psychics, readers of palms, tea leaves and the stars. It may have been this that also took her to Tally's Kinema, shortly after being given the *Four Horsemen* project, to see *Eyes of Youth*. Although she may have felt slighted to find that crystal-ball gazing, so prominently featured in all of the ads, was little more than an ingenious plot device to spin off three stories with the same character, there was something else in the movie that brought her back to see the film again and again. It was a young actor in the third episode, whose impeccable attire and immaculate grooming emphasized the exotic. He seemed to exude an electric quality that touched upon suppressed desires. But it would not be until some weeks later, mulling over the problem of casting for *The Four Horsemen,* that June would realize that she had found her Julio Desnoyers.

In Ibañez's broad, sweeping novel about two families descended from a wealthy Argentine landowner, the role of Julio Desnoyers is but one among a large cast of characters. Following the death of the patriarch, the families divide his wealth. One family, the Desnoyers, moves to France, while the other, the von Hartotts, moves to Germany. Thus the stage is set for the eventual conflict between Julio Desnoyers and his cousin on a French battlefield. The characterization of Julio is that of a spoiled, arrogant, dilettante, who gets involved in an affair with a young married woman and finds redemption just before his death in battle.

Richard Rowland, receiving a nod of approval from June, asked Rudolph how much he was being paid by Selznick for his work on *The Wonderful Chance*.

"Four hundred a week," said the actor.

Rowland, figuring he was being bluffed, made a counter bluff, "This will be a small part and we're tightly budgeted. I'll pay you three-fifty."

Rudolph frowned for a short moment before accepting.

Rowland smiled as they shook hands. If anything, the risks that were being taken on *The Four Horsemen* —the use of relatively unknown talent on a war film with a woman at the helm—were being minimized by his shrewd dealings. Although he had given up a good percentage of the profit when purchasing the screen rights, that was hypothetical money. In "cash in hand" he had saved Metro ten thousand dollars on the upfront price and now by keeping salaries and costs low the picture stood a good chance of making a profit.

Within the following year, Rowland would come to rue his attempts to economize during Metro's hard days. The ten thousand saved could be multiplied by forty to equal what would be paid out to Ibañez in percentages.

And, his low salaries would eventually lead to the loss of a star and his screen writer.

The Four Horsemen was to become the product of powerful energies and extraordinary talent fused together by creative teamwork. Director Rex Ingram, another "young unknown" discovered by June, rehearsed his actors to perfection before permitting the camera to swing into play. John Seitz's cameras would eloquently capture the mood and passions involved. June Mathis had developed the innovative technique of "shooting on paper"—a term applied to preconceiving the position of the camera and its moves while writing the scenario. Working with director Alberto Capellani, she introduced Ingram to this technique and proved an invaluable coordinator. Later she would work closely with the film cutters in editing and adding printed dialogue to the film.

Meanwhile, Valentino, bringing a burning intensity to his work, found himself being orchestrated by Mathis and Ingram. "No, no Rudy. You're not playing to the third balcony. Tone down the gesture. Remember, the camera is an intimate thing." For the first time, he began to realize that acting for the screen did not involve the exaggerated movements that he had used previously. The craft lay in subtle things: a movement of the hand, a fleeting expression. In the screening room where the rushes were shown, excitement grew. June and Ingram conferred daily, changing the thrust of the story by rewriting the script to amplify the role of Julio Desnoyers.

Their excitement overflowed to the set, permeating the cast and crew. The realization that they were involved in a potential hit sparked them all, and the actors stretched their abilities. It wasn't long before the "dailies," as the rushes were called, began to fill the tiny screening room with studio executives and staff. It was to them that growing awareness came. A star was being born.

New scenes were written for Julio Desnoyers. Old scenes were scrapped. Soon it was the leading role in the film. The affair between the married woman, Marguerite Laurier, and Julio was given more screen time.

Ingram could hardly have been more pleased. He was deeply in love with Alice Terry who played Marguerite, and as Rudolph's role was enlarged, so was Alice's. Finally, Dick Rowland untied the pursestrings and more money became available to permit breathtaking scenes with hundreds of extras. Eventually, the cost of the movie would rise to $600,000.

Rudolph was not unaware of what was happening. Studio executives and other Metro stars who had previously ignored him began stopping by his table at the studio commissary to chat. Extras and secretaries would smile at him and many girls flirted openly. A new world was opening, and the view was thrilling.

When the shooting on *The Four Horsemen* had been completed, he was rushed into another film to capitalize on his success. Called *Uncharted Seas,* it was a rather flimsy tale about gold-seekers in Alaska. Rudolph asked Karger for a raise and was turned down. The rejection nettled Valentino who had heard that his co-star, Alice Lake, was earning $1,200 a week.

Meantime, June Mathis had moved on to work with the studio's top star, the great Nazimova, in the pre-production phase of *Camille.* With Nazimova playing the title role, a search was being made for the role of her lover, Armand. June suggested Valentino. Nazimova had heard the advance raves about his performance in *The Four Horsemen,* but she was still hesitant. June arranged for a private screening of the love scenes between Valentino and Alice Terry, and the Russian actress was impressed.

"Have the young man come see me and after I talk with him I will introduce him to Natacha. If we both agree that he will make a good Armand, he will be hired," she declared.

When Valentino was informed that Nazimova was willing to meet with him, he had just finished two hours of shooting for *Uncharted Seas* in the hot sun while dressed in heavy furs. Having set aside her once vehement dislike for the young man involved in the De Saulles affair, Nazimova spoke with him briefly. Pleased, she took him to see her assistant.

Standing beside a desk, studying a series of sketches

of costumes, was a woman who was, physically, Nazimova's opposite. Nazimova was short, with a head too large for her body. This woman was tall, slim and graceful. Her hair was straight, curled into a bun which she wore aside her head. Her facial features were well chiseled, with high cheekbones. Nazimova kept her temperament on constant display. This woman was more than self-contained—her demeanor was almost frigid.

Nazimova made the introductions. "Rudy, I want you to meet the person who designs my sets, costumes and makes my artistic decisions, Natacha Rambova."

What Natacha saw before her was considerably less than she had been led to expect. The meeting was brief. Rudolph had to be back on his set.

Later, when the decision that he had been selected to play Armand was made known to him, he was jubilant. He asked if it had been because of Natacha's recommendation. No, he was told. Nazimova had insisted.

It may have been his male ego—the challenge of melting this iceberg. It may have been the curious fascination that Natacha held for him. But Rudolph was prompted to ask her to accompany him to a masquerade ball. To his delight she accepted.

Rudolph soon found that Natacha was an excellent dancer, having once been associated with a Russian dance troupe. They discovered mutual interests in literature, music and the arts. The loneliness of their private lives was glimpsed. There was now an affinity between them.

The starting date for production on *Camille* was set back three weeks to await Valentino's availability. Alice Lake agreed to allow changes in the shooting schedule so that the scenes involving him would be shot first.

The Four Horsemen of the Apocalypse received its world premiere at the Lyric Theater in New York on May 6, 1921. At its end, the opening night audience rose to their feet applauding. The movie which had been brought into being by a woman screenwriter with a group of unknowns was on its way to becoming a part of screen history.

Among those in the first night audience were Adolph Zukor and Jesse Lasky. Lasky was so impressed by Valentino's performance—"every movement has the lithe grace of a panther," he said—that he sent the actor a warm congratulatory letter.

Natacha accompanied Valentino to the Los Angeles opening a week later. The rave notices from New York had already cued the audience that they were about to view a movie masterpiece. They were not disappointed. During the middle of the film, Natacha felt Rudolph take her hand which he began to squeeze tightly as tears came to his eyes and hers. As in New York, the end of the film brought the audience to their feet applauding, as many dabbed at their eyes with handkerchiefs. Rudolph found himself surrounded and congratulated by his peers in the industry, many of whom had snubbed him previously.

While Hollywood has a tradition of overnight fame, never before had a single picture elevated five people into its sanctified hierarchy. Metro, who would be grossing over four million dollars from *The Four Horsemen* in the next few years, immediately signed the quintet for another film. The vehicle was a screen version of Balzac's novel, *Eugenie Grandet,* with the provocative title, *The Conquering Power.* Rex Ingram, who had received most of the credit for the success of *The Four Horsemen,* was hired not only to direct but to be in charge of the production. June Mathis was given the screen adaptation chores, John Seitz placed in charge of photography, and by popular demand Metro brought back the stars, Rudolph Valentino and Alice Terry, now Mrs. Rex Ingram.

Once production began, Rudolph spoke to June Mathis about a strong source of aggravation and concern to him. This was his third film since *The Four Horsemen,* but he had not been given a raise in salary from $350 a week. His new star status was worth more than that. June agreed that he should receive at least a hundred dollars more a week and took Rudolph's complaint to Rex Ingram. Ingram refused. Rudolph finally settled for a fifty-dollar raise.

All the young principals from *The Four Horsemen*

had fallen victim to the star syndrome. In Valentino's case, Natacha was a contributory cause. She had been behind the wage demand—having been astounded when she learned how little the actor who had given flesh to Ibañez's Julio Desnoyers was earning. Noting slights by the studio and by others toward Rudolph, she insisted that he stand up for his rights. Her basis of comparison was the treatment and salary accorded Nazimova—a comparison not completely equitable.

If the making of *The Four Horsemen* could be likened to a symphony with each artist contributing toward the melody, the set of *The Conquering Power* was utter cacophony as individuals competed against each other to fatten their personal glories.

In one scene, Rudolph was dressed in formal evening attire. Suddenly, in midscene, Ingram called for the action to stop and began to berate his star for being improperly dressed. "Dammit," he said, "you're wearing a white vest. I thought you were supposed to be a fashion plate."

Ingram could not have aimed at a more sensitive target. If there was one thing that Valentino prided himself on, it was his appearance. (Dorothy Gish once remarked that she would have used Valentino in films after *Out of Luck* had it not been for the long time it took him to dress.)

Valentino, hurt by Ingram's remark in front of his fellow players and the crew, snapped back angrily, "You're crazy in the head! Besides, what do you know about fashion. All you ever wear is that ugly trench coat and knickers!"

As extras watched—many of them obviously amused —a verbal battle ensued. Ingram insisted on his directorial rights. "I don't want any back talk, Valentino. I'm the boss on this set and if I tell you to take a flying jump in the lake with those clothes, I expect you to do it!"

"If the script says for me to jump in the lake, I'll do it. But the scene calls for me to be dressed properly and I won't dress like a dumbbell just because of your stupidity!"

To avoid fisticuffs between a director who had been a flying ace in the war and an actor who prided himself for his athletic skills as well as his personal wardrobe, John Seitz stepped between them and persuaded the two to accept the decision of an authority. Frank Elliot, an English actor and fashion plate, was mutually accepted by both parties as a qualified expert. Elliot agreed with Valentino. "I would find a black vest to be absolutely ridiculous," he said.

Neither took the decision well. Valentino appeared to gloat. Ingram became surly. During the rest of the scene Ingram refused to direct his male star and would not look into the camera to check the framing as he always did before each shooting. Instead, after calling for "action and camera," he turned his back to the set. Cleaning his nails with a penknife, he carried on a conversation with his assistants.

When *The Conquering Power* was in the can, technicians and bit players alike sighed with relief. The tensions that had hovered daily over the set had affected them all. And when the film opened in New York it would be unanimously panned. Valentino, however, emerged almost unscathed. *The New York Times* called him "a pantomimist of marked ability."

During shooting on *The Conquering Power,* Metro had held a reception for the *enfant terrible* of the French moviemakers, Abel Gance. After the reception, Gance's spectacular three-hour epic, *J'accuse,* was screened. Metro was anxious to hire the young Frenchman and had offered him a contract starting at $3,000 a week for the first year with a thousand dollars a week raise beginning the second year.

J'accuse, like *The Four Horsemen,* was a powerful indictment of war. Unlike the American film, it had been practically a one-man effort. Gance, who had started his career as a playwright, had written the script, directed, and been in charge of photography. Shooting the film during the end of World War I, Gance actually took his cameras onto the battlefield. Aside from the principals, the actors were real soldiers. When his cameras moved in for close-ups, the tired, empty expressions that the lens captured were those that few actors could have possibly imitated so authentically.

After the Hollywood screening, Gance joined Valentino, Natacha and Nazimova for a drink. In a sense it was a gathering of Europeans since the only American at the table, Natacha, had spent much of her life in Europe. And the conversation, spoken in French, centered on the European motion picture industry.

Valentino had been enormously moved by Gance's film. It had brought into focus the frustration he felt. "I would give anything to work with you," he told Gance. "I am tired of this place. I can't stand the atmosphere. It is too artificial."

Natacha joined in. "Success here is measured by box-office receipts. Everyone here tries to make movies as quickly and as cheaply as possible. No one cares about a film's intellectual or artistic merit."

Gance nodded. He mentioned that Metro had offered him a contract—which he would be turning down. He reasoned that he would have to sell out his freedom for the Metro money. "My methods of working differ from the American formula of making films," he said. "In order to make a film like *J'accuse,* one has to be completely independent."

It was an important evening for Rudolph. Abel Gance's words had fortified convictions that were crystallizing in him. Abel Gance's philosophy of filmmaking became his.

In a small studio, as Metro was, the grapevine was far more efficient than Western Union. During the daily phone conversations with the New York office, Valentino's problems with Ingram had been reported on a blow-by-blow basis. In a situation between a $1,000 a week director and a $400 a week actor, the studio invariably sided with the director. Disrespect toward authority from the ranks of temperamental stars was considered intolerable. This being the case, it was not altogether surprising that following *The Conquering Power,* Metro seemed to have temporarily run out of roles for Rudolph. There was something else afoot, too. Productions were being cut back because Richard

VALENTINO:
The Eternal Lover

50th Anniversary of Valentino's Death

The mysterious "Lady in Black" at the 50th Anniversary of Valentino's death, August 23, 1976. A thousand mourners gathered for the memorial service in Hollywood.

Genesis

Rodolfo Guglielmi
as a child, circa 1904.

Rodolfo, age 17,
at Royal Agriculture
Academy near Genoa, Italy.
Valentino is on left.

Rodolfo, December 1913,
aboard the SS <u>Cleveland</u>,
immigrating to the
United States from Italy.

A
Society
Sensation

Top: As a dancer at Maxim's, Rodolfo put
much of his earnings into fine clothes.

Bottom: As Rodolfo di Valentina, he appeared on
vaudeville stages as a dancer in 1915-1916.

"Eyes of Youth"

Valentino with Mae Murray in a scene from
"The Delicious Little Devil," 1919.

Left: Valentino had hoped for the role of the
Chinese lover in D. W. Griffith's "Broken Blossoms,"
but lost it to top star Richard Barthelmess. After seeing
the film he posed for a number of publicity portraits in
costume, hoping for such a great role. This is an example.

Below: Valentino and Dorothy Gish in a scene from
"Out of Luck," 1919. He played the "heavy," as usual.

Valentino with Clara Kimball Young in a scene
from "Eyes of Youth," 1919. This film brought him
to the attention of June Mathis, and eventually to the
lead in "The Four Horsemen of the Apocalypse,"
the film which brought him stardom.

The
Big Break

Top: A scene from "The Conquering Power," 1921.
Bottom: Valentino and Nazimova in "Camille," 1921.

Top: Natacha Rambova, Valentino's second wife.

Bottom: Rudolph and Natacha in a quiet off-set moment during the filming of "Camille."

Assembled on one of the lavish interior sets of
"The Four Horsemen of the Apocalypse" were the principals
from the film. Surrounding director Rex Ingram, seated
foreground, are cameraman John Seitz, right of Ingram;
Alice Terry, Valentino, and June Mathis, on floor.

Valentino as the gaucho in
"The Four Horsemen of the Apocalypse," 1921.

"The Sheik"

Famous publicity portrait of Valentino as "The Sheik," 1921.

The famous seduction scene in "The Sheik," with Agnes Ayres.

In the sheik's tent.

Valentino's major avocation was photography,
a hobby he pursued with zeal. Here, he is
photographing Natacha in Palm Springs.

Top: Rudolph and Natacha in a rare scrapbook photograph taken prior to their marriage.

Bottom: Valentino and Natacha on their first wedding day in Mexicali, Mexico, May 13, 1922.

The
Conquering
Hero

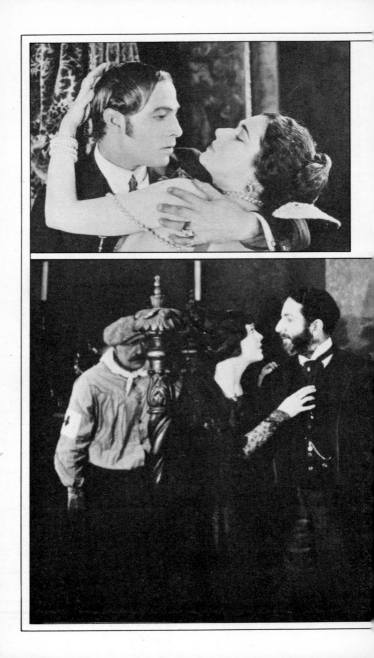

Left: Succumbing to the wiles of vamp
Nita Naldi in "Blood and Sand," his embrace
was passionate and his eyes soulful.

Below: The death scene in "Blood and Sand," 1922.
Lila Lee is shown as the wife.

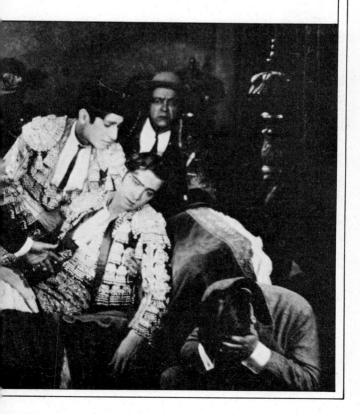

Valentino during fencing rehearsal for "Young Rajah," 1922.

Jean Acker, Rudolph Valentino's first wife,
seen during press interview on January 10, 1922, the day
Valentino was awarded interlocutory divorce decree.

Right: Rudolph and Natacha Rambova Valentino, about the time of their second marriage in March, 1923. Published in <u>Photoplay</u> in April, 1923, this portrait raised a few eyebrows.

Below: After the bigamy trial, and while Valentino was waiting out the divorce decree from Jean Acker, he posed for a series of photographs for <u>Photoplay</u> magazine depicting the loneliness of living without Natacha. Here, alone in the Whitley Heights house.

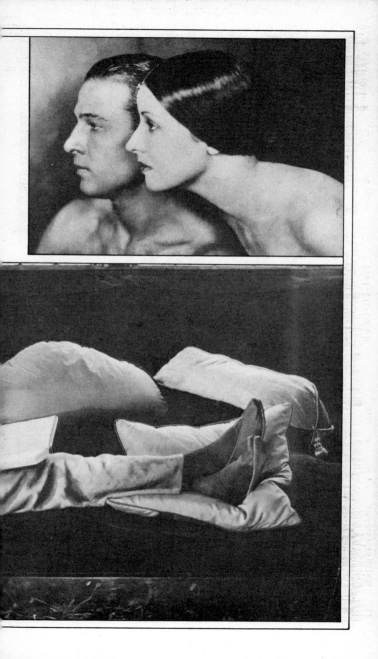

Rudy and Natacha outside their Whitley Heights home. Natacha is holding one of her Pekinese dogs; Rudy is with Prince, his German Shepherd.

Going Home

Rudolph Valentino and Natacha at the Juan les Pins
(France) villa owned by Natacha's mother and
stepfather, Mr. and Mrs. Richard Hudnut.

Rudy and Natacha pose during their first trip
to Europe together in the summer of 1923.

The
Break Up

Top: Rudy and Natacha arriving in America after their second European trip in January, 1924.

Bottom: Valentino in "A Sainted Devil," 1924.

Top: Valentino in a portrait that was to have been used
for "The Hooded Falcon," a film that was never made.

Bottom: The epitome of controlled ardor, fingers
bedecked with rings, he draws Doris Kenyon to
his lips in "Monsieur Beaucaire," 1924.

Top: Action scene from "Monsieur Beaucaire."
Bottom: Valentino and Vilma Banky in "The Eagle," 1925.

Valentino in a costume from "The Eagle."

Top: The last farewell as Natacha poses with Valentino at the Pasadena railroad station as she leaves for New York. This marked the end of their marriage.

Bottom: As Valentino's marriage to Natacha was ending, he was again able to spend time with his male friends.

Top: Valentino spent many hours working on his cars.

Bottom: Valentino, aboard the <u>Leviathan</u>, departing New York on his last trip to Europe, November 14, 1925, alone.

Valentino, alone, in their Whitley Heights house
after Natacha left him. Later, he moved to
Falcon's Lair, early fall, 1925.

Uncharted
Seas

Valentino and Pola Negri at the premier of "The Son of the Sheik."

Top: Valentino and Vilma Banky in "The Son of the Sheik."

Bottom: Vilma Banky, this time as the
dancing girl Yasmin, is swept up by Valentino
who kidnapped her in "The Son of the Sheik."

A memorable photograph taken in late spring 1926 shows
Valentino and Pola Negri sitting on fence at extreme right.
Next to Valentino is Jack Pickford, Mary's brother. At
extreme left on fence is Roscoe "Fatty" Arbuckle with Mae
Murray next to him. Richard Barthelmess, at whose birth-
day party this was taken, is standing left center in a

white sweatshirt. Ronald Colman is seated on fence directly above him. To the right of Barthelmess are Constance Talmadge and Beatrice Lillie. Louella Parsons is third from the left, standing in middle row. Howard Hughes is at the extreme right of the picture.

Top: Valentino and Pola Negri at a costume party at the Ambassador Hotel, Los Angeles, in 1926. Valentino wears a costume from "Blood and Sand."

Bottom: Valentino regularly did calisthenics to keep in shape.

Death
and
Aftermath

One of the last portraits of Valentino, made in 1926 by famed photographer Henry Waxman, and inscribed in French to Pola—"Polita."

The crowd outside Campbell's Funeral Church.

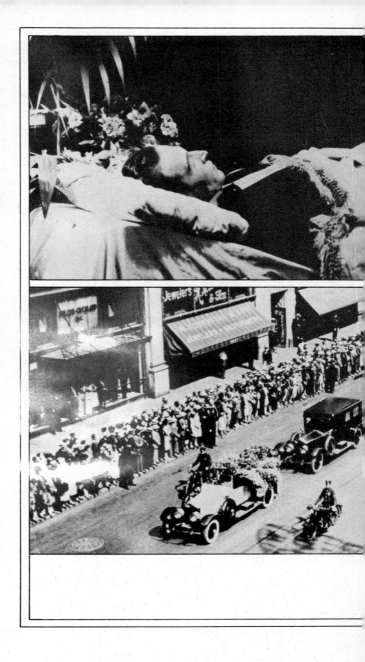

Top: Valentino's body at Campbell's Funeral Church
in New York, August 24-29, 1926.

Bottom: Crowds lined the streets as the funeral cortege moved past
Broadway and 44th Street, New York City, August 30, 1926.

Valentino's Death Certificate, 1926, showing "gastric ulcer and general peritonitis" as the primary causes of death, and "septic pneumonia and septic endocarditis" as contributory causes.

Sons of
"The Sheik"

One of the many imitative films made by others after Valentino's success in "The Sheik." Here, Ramon Navarro and Alice Terry in "The Arab."

Another imitative film was "Chu Chin Chow" with Frederic Norton and Betty Blythe.

The comics of the Twenties did not hesitate to satirize Valentino films. Here, Ben Turpin in his version of "The Sheik."

One of the most
successful of the Valentino
imitators, Antonio Moreno.

In 1951, producer Edward Small
and Columbia Pictures released
their version of a Valentino
biography, "Valentino," starring
Valentino look-alike Anthony
Dexter and Eleanor Parker.

Top: In 1975, Spelling-Goldberg's "The Legend of Valentino" appeared nationally on ABC-Television. Franco Nero portrayed Valentino.

Bottom: In 1977, United Artists has scheduled for release a major production by director Ken Russell called "Valentino," starring Russian ballet star Rudolf Nureyev. Here, Nureyev, portraying Valentino, is shown recreating a scene from "Blood and Sand."

The One
and Only
Sheik

Rowland was in the process of turning over control of Metro to the theater tycoon, Marcus Loew. A short time after his acquisition of the studio, Loew fed two million dollars from the profits of his theater chain into Metro to make good its losses. Fortunately, *The Four Horsemen* was bringing back its investment and more.

At liberty, Rudolph spent a lot of time with Natacha, who was also not working. After completing *A Society Sensation* three years before, Rudolph had rushed out and purchased a $750 Mercer runabout for a hundred dollars down and fifty dollars a month. Not long thereafter, during lean times, the auto dealer repossessed the car. Since then, Valentino had been wary of car salesmen. When he needed a car, he could always borrow one, or a friend would give him a ride. And as he became a regular visitor in Natacha's home, he gradually took over the use of her secondhand Buick runabout. For all practical purposes, it soon became his.

But there was a problem with Natacha's Buick: it had no pick-up. One day he took it out and returned with a much older, dilapidated hulk of a car. It was a 1914 Cadillac. Enthusiastically, Rudolph told Natacha of the great bargain he had made. He had traded the Buick for the Cadillac and received four hundred dollars in cash! As for the age and the looks of the car, he said, those matters were of minor importance. What was important was the size and power of the Cadillac's engine, and it was in great shape. To celebrate, they dressed in their finest and took the Cadillac into Santa Monica where, for the first time in the current series of lean days, they ate an expensive dinner that began with champagne and ended with cognac.

On the way back, they learned that while the car had a frightening amount of power, it also had a remarkable ability to consume gas and oil. A few blocks from Natacha's house, the car had to be abandoned until a gas station opened the next day so that its empty tank could be refilled.

The old adage "penny-wise and pound foolish" describes Natacha and Rudolph's attitude toward money. When they had a lot, it was spent extravagantly. And when things were tight, they both knew from experience how to survive on very little. After the remainder of the four hundred dollars from the car trade was spent, the two adjusted their living habits accordingly. The first light of dawn would find them in the open country outside Santa Monica, Natacha at the wheel of the Cadillac, with its top down, and Rudolph sitting on top of the cowling that covered the folded-down roof, shotgun in hand, his narrowed eyes searching for quail or rabbits. At other times, they hunted mussels among the rocks of the Pacific.

This would be the leanest period for them, but it was filled with the joys of small pleasures. The future stretched before them—everything was to be gained and very little lost.

Meanwhile, Rudolph looked for work. The responses had been "I'll keep you in mind," or "I'll give you a call." It was Natacha who forced him into dropping in on Jesse Lasky. "Look," she said, "the problem is you've been speaking to guys in the middle. Why not go see the guys at the top."

When Rudolph answered that he didn't know many top brass people, Natacha reminded him, "What about the letter from Lasky? Why don't you tell him you were around the studio visiting old friends and dropped in to thank him."

"I'll do it tomorrow," he promised. That evening in his apartment, he spent hours picking out the most conservative suit, the proper shirt and tie, the right handkerchief to wear in his jacket pocket. He then polished and repolished his shoes.

Lasky received him after only a few minutes wait. "Rudolph," he said, a broad smile breaking across his face as the light reflected from his pince-nez. "How nice of you to drop by. I so admired your work in *The Four Horsemen.*"

Rudolph explained that he had been seeing friends and wanted to thank him for the letter. They laughed and chatted. Then, Rudolph asked if Famous Players-Lasky had any productions coming up that might include a part for him.

Lasky could not hide his disbelief. "You mean that

Metro doesn't have an option on your future services?"

Rudolph said no. Karger, he said, had offered him a contract at $400 a week but he had refused it.

"How much did you want?" Lasky asked.

"Four-fifty," Rudolph replied.

Lasky was stunned. He had heard stories about Ingram's problems with Valentino and there were rumors that the *Four Horsemen* star was getting difficult to handle. But that Karger would let Valentino walk out of his office unsigned because of fifty dollars a week didn't seem to make sense.

Lasky offered Rudolph a five-year contract with options. The starting salary would be $500 a week. In order to keep Valentino from going around shopping for a better price, he offered a bonus of one week's salary if he was willing to sign right away. Rudolph agreed and signed.

During the conversation that followed, Lasky learned that June Mathis was also unhappy at Metro. She had expected her success in handling *The Four Horsemen* to put her in charge of other productions. Yet, she had only been given a small raise and her role had reverted to what it had been before. And, in her last two films, she had had to work under Nazimova and Rex Ingram—the director she had discovered.

After Valentino left, Lasky got June on the phone. She was receptive to making a change. June was delighted to hear that Valentino had signed with the biggest studio in Hollywood and was excited about the possibility of working on a story for him. She would drop by and discuss terms.

It had been a good day for Jesse Lasky. He buzzed his secretary and asked her to come in. He began dictating a letter to his executives informing them that he had hired the star of *The Four Horsemen* and asking them to come up with possible stories. His secretary, Jeane Cohen, interrupted him. "But Mr. Lasky, you have a story that would be right for him. Remember *The Sheik?*"

Several months earlier, Jeane Cohen had insisted that Lasky read the story by Edith M. Hull. She felt it would make a good movie. Lasky never read books. What he would read were two-page synopses of books prepared by his $25-a-week readers. To appease Jeane he had one of the women readers read the book and tell him about it. Seeing its possibilities, he checked with director George Melford, who also liked it. He bought the screen rights to *The Sheik* for $12,500 before realizing that he had no one under contract who would be right to play a savage desert chieftain.

Now he was doubly elated. The olive-skinned Italian, his skin darkened a bit, would be ideal for the role. Lasky also remembered that the studio owned another book that would be right for Valentino, Ibañez's novel about a matador, *Blood and Sand*. He felt jubilant. When June Mathis came in, he would be able to offer her two exciting stories to work on. How could she refuse?

THE MARRIED VIRGIN

Natacha Rambova was born Winifred Shaunessy in Salt Lake City in 1897.

Winifred grew up a quiet child, fond of drawing pictures and fascinated by butterflies. She never made friends easily and after her parents divorced she withdrew even more into herself. When she had just entered her teens, her mother remarried—quite well. For the man who became Winifred's stepfather was Richard Hudnut, the cosmetic king. Within the year, Winifred was shipped off to a private school in England and from there to the School of Fine Arts in Paris. When she was seventeen she began studying ballet under Theodore Kosloff and was soon accepted into his Imperial Russian Ballet Corps, taking the name Natacha Rambova. When the Kosloff troupe ended its American tour in Los Angeles in 1917, she was its premiere danseuse. At a party she met the actress Nazimova and the two had an instant rapport, communicating as they did in three languages—Russian, French and English. When news of the revolution in Russia reached Kosloff, he disbanded his troupe. Natacha decided to join Nazimova as the art director on her films.

The exact nature of their private relationship will probably never be known, although the close bond between them during working hours often lent itself to conjecture. Nazimova's preference for the company of young women was fairly well known within the industry.

There was no softness or confusion about Natacha. Every step she took had a purpose. Product of a broken marriage, set adrift in private schools abroad, Natacha

61

had learned very early not merely to succeed but to exceed. Her achievement in becoming the premier danseuse at the age of twenty was not due to ability alone. She was tougher, more compulsively driven, and her claws were longer and sharper than the other female dancers in the corps de ballet.

On their first date to the masquerade ball, she was prepared to dislike Rudolph. She found that the tough, menacing Julio from the pampas was in reality a gentle, attentive male. They danced—and she had never found so graceful a partner. But were the emotions that moved within her sexual or maternal?

When her man-child came to her after his meeting with Lasky, she shared his joy until second thoughts made her suspicious. "Why was he so anxious to have you sign right then and there?" she said. "That old fox! He knew you could get more elsewhere! Rudy! You should have asked for a thousand. He knows you're worth more!"

The actor's jubilation turned to doubt. Yes, it had been too quick and easy. The reel rewound in his mind and the scene played back. He saw Lasky's smile of greeting again; the executive had been delighted to see him. He recalled Lasky's surprise to find out what Karger's offer had been. Within minutes, Rudolph's image of Lasky had changed from that of a kind benefactor to a shrewd exploiter. Valentino's attitude toward the studios and the men who ruled them would never again be the same.

When he learned that his first endeavor for Famous Players-Lasky would be *The Sheik,* he felt much better. Sheik Ahmed Ben Hassan was the romantic, dashing hero of his day dreams. Natacha did not share his enthusiasm. "The story is tripe," she said. "It's nothing more than a dime-store novel."

June Mathis, who had signed with Lasky, must have shared Natacha's views. After several attempts, she threw up her hands and begged off the writing project. It just wasn't her type of story, she told Lasky.

Without Mathis or Ingram to guide him, the portrayal of the savage desert chieftain became almost entirely Rudolph's invention. He instilled within the role all of the powerful male characteristics he had learned to dam up within himself since his days as a gigolo. If his depiction was an overstatement, it was an overstatement that the newly emancipated women of the nation would thrive on. Women were to find in *The Sheik* a symbol of the omnipotent male who could dominate them as the men in their own lives could not. The pervading theme of sado-masochism in Valentino's performance grasped tightly at their libidos.

The eventual success of the film which was to skyrocket the one-time bit part villain into screen immortality as the Great Lover would come as a surprise to the studio. The opening titles gave Valentino second billing after Agnes Ayers.

In late October and November 1921, when the film was released across the nation, theaters soon filled to capacity with audiences composed primarily of women. Long lines queued up before each performance. The mailroom of Famous Players-Lasky was soon besieged with letters—more than a thousand a week—addressed to Rudolph Valentino. Many bore lipstick imprints of a kiss. Requests for pictures, autographs and proposals of love—many very explicit—poured in. The studio called back prints of the movie and issued new ones with titles placing Valentino's name above Agnes Ayers'.

Front page headlines in November were full of developments in Fatty Arbuckle's trial for the death of Virginia Rappe. During a wild party in a suite at San Francisco's prestigious St. Francis hotel, gallons of illicit hooch had turned the festivities into a veritable bacchanalia. It came to a frightening halt when Arbuckle emerged from a bedroom where Virginia was found dying of a ruptured bladder. The reaction of the nation to Arbuckle was so violent that all of his movies were withdrawn. Though he was acquitted after three trials, Arbuckle's career was permanently ended.

Arbuckle was Famous Players-Lasky's top comedian and the studio was caught up in the trial when a new headline appeared. Valentino, its newest star, was being sued for separate maintenance, $300 a month and $1,500 for attorney fees by his wife, Jean Acker. Valentino, in a counter-suit, had filed for divorce. On November 23, Jean testified that after returning from location where she had been working on an Arbuckle movie, she was taking a bath when Valentino broke into her apartment and began hammering on the bathroom door, threatening to break it down unless she opened it. When she did, an argument ensued and, "He hit me with his fist and knocked me down . . . I cried and my face got red and puffy . . . He begged forgiveness . . . and then he told me he didn't want to be married to me any longer and intimated that he'd like to have me frame up some divorce evidence. I refused . . . He said he would always be my dear friend but he didn't want to be my husband. 'I have a future and I don't want any woman hampering my career.'" The following day, being out of funds, she asked him for money. "He said he'd *loan* me money but he wouldn't *give* me a penny."

In the days that followed, Grace Darmond testified that she was in her apartment at the time of the fight and could hear the commotion in Jean's apartment, which was next to hers. At one point, she said, she heard the sound of somebody hitting the floor. The Kargers both took the stand and told of Jean coming to their home some six hours after the marriage, "She thought she had made a mistake and threw herself on the bed and wept."

Douglas Gerrard testified in behalf of his friend. He described Valentino's grief and bewilderment. He also brought forth a telegram he'd received from Jean when she went on location to Lone Pine: "RUDOLPH THREATENS TO SEE ME. KEEP HIM AWAY. I DON'T WANT HIM HERE."

On the last day of November, a new name was brought into the trial. On December 1, the *Los Angeles Examiner* reported: "A little oval picture, somewhat startling to say the least, showing Rudolph Valentino, noted film star, and Natacha Rambova, former dancer and art director, was injected into the case. But Valentino said the picture was merely in preparation for a new play." While none of the newspapers described the contents of the photograph, writers have suggested that the picture showed the couple in a compromising situation. It is known that Valentino, while posing for a series of semi-nude photographs inspired by those of the great dancer Nijinsky in *The Afternoon of a Faun,* had also posed for at least one picture in which Natacha was included.

Valentino testified that Natacha had been a friend for some time and had helped him by taking care of his fan mail. "These letters Miss Rambova took care of by turning them over to her maid to answer." In addition, he said, he consulted with her regarding the art work on his pictures and that he had never had to pay her for her help.

On January 10, 1922, two years precisely to the date when, according to Jean, Valentino had burst into her apartment to strike her, Judge Thomas O. Toland provided Rudolph with an interlocutory divorce from Jean Acker.

During the course of the trial which was ending one marriage, Rudolph was preparing for another. Pooling their money, he and Natacha bought a house on Wedgewood Place in Whitley Heights. It was a two-level Spanish-style stucco building that hugged the side of a hill overlooking Highland Avenue on one side and Cahuenga on the other. Beyond Highland was the bowl-shaped valley that had just been named the Hollywood Bowl.

Natacha moved into the house two days before Christmas with the scant furnishings from her tiny bungalow. Here on Christmas Eve, in a living room occupied only by a Christmas tree and one chair, they lit candles on the tree at midnight. As Natacha began to open their presents, Rudolph directed her to the bedroom. Closing the door, he instructed her not to come out until he called. Ten minutes later, after Rudolph returned from his home with a friend down the hill, she heard the front door slam and Rudolph's footsteps on the floor below. She called down and received no response. She called again. This time she heard a tiny, muffled bark. She raced down the stairs and there, peering from the top of one of her stockings, were the head and two paws of a tiny Pekinese puppy.

In the meantime Rudolph went to work on his second film for Lasky, *Moran of the Lady Letty,* a seafaring story adapted from a Frank Norris novel. On the set he was greeted by old friends and new. George Melford was directing, Monte Katterjohn had written the scenario and his co-star was Dorothy Dalton.

Immediately following *Moran,* Rudolph was rushed into *Beyond the Rocks* with Gloria Swanson, the highest ranking queen of Famous Players-Lasky. Gloria, who was commanding a salary of $12,500 a week from the Zukor-Lasky combine—which was in the process of changing its name to Paramount—had a contract stipulating that her name alone would be placed above the title of any film in which she appeared. Natacha, who had taken over Valentino's managerial reins, insisted that Rudolph be given co-starring credit. Lasky was forced to call Gloria to obtain her approval.

Gloria was all sweetness. "It's all right if you want to put his name above the title below mine, Mr. Lasky. But if I allow you to do that, I think you should have the studio send me on a trip to Europe at the studio's expense." Lasky, caught in a squeeze, was forced to agree.

Had the request come from any other actor, it is doubtful that Gloria would have been as generous—regardless of what might have been offered in exchange. She had liked Rudolph, however, since the first time they'd met some years before.

Queen that she was, Swanson was not above a good practical joke. Valentino's love for the favorite herb of the Italians, the *allium sativum,* better known as garlic, had been the dismay of many leading ladies who had worked opposite him, despite his use of perfumes to cloak the aroma. Swanson, annoyed by being on the downwind side, especially in the clinches, decided to retaliate in style.

In *Beyond the Rocks,* Rudolph discovers a handkerchief left behind by the lady he loves. The action called for him to pick up the perfumed hanky, bring it to his nostrils and inhale the scent as his expression turns to bliss. In the run-through, Valentino played the scene with all the ardor he possessed. Director San

Wood, satisfied, called for a "take." Following Swanson's instructions, the prop man substituted a handkerchief immersed in garlic juice. This time, as the rolling film caught every subtle nuance of expression, Valentino sniffed deeply of the delicate bit of lace and recorded one of the most horrendous expressions ever seen. Gloria, seated by the camera, laughed until tears streamed from her eyes—necessitating an hour's delay while her makeup was washed off and reapplied.

For *Moran,* Valentino's salary was raised to seven hundred a week, and for *Rocks* he was paid an even thousand. Then Paramount agreed to put him into the role he wanted most of all, *Blood and Sand,* at a salary of $1,500 a week.

By now Valentino believed he had learned how the game was played: power begets power. He asked for and was given June Mathis to write the screen adaptation from Vicent Blasco Ibañez's novel. He wanted his choice of directors, George Fitzmaurice, the Frenchman with whom he had recently developed a great rapport. Further, he asked that the film be shot on location in Spain.

Lasky agreed to Fitzmaurice—if he was available. As for Spain, it was a good idea but out of the question. When Valentino insisted, Lasky said he would check with Zukor to see if the budget would permit some location work in Spain. "Do you know the kind of problems you're asking for, Rudy? The crew will have language, food and living problems and the costs will be enormous. For example, suppose you need trained extras or even carpenters, how can you find them right away?"

Rudolph, having been goaded by Natacha to stand up for his rights, let loose. The problem with the studio, he said, was that they were concerned only with money. In Europe, when Gance wanted to film a war movie, he had gone to the war. Similarly, if Paramount wanted to do a story on a Spanish matador, they should go to Spain where the backgrounds were, and not the outlands of Hollywood or a studio back lot.

Then he added what was, for him, the clincher. He had long suspected, he said—and now Natacha had borne him out, that he was possessed of psychic powers. "It is the heart of my acting," he said. "I can stand at Santa Monica Boulevard and King's Road where fifty years ago they captured the great Mexican bandit Vasquez, and feel how he felt when trapped by the sheriff. It is the same when I touch an object or wear a costume from a certain period—I am taken to that period. It was so when I went into the hills at home where the Greeks hid from the Romans. I knew how they thought, how they felt."

Lasky, when he spoke to Zukor about Valentino's demands, would mention this psychic power that the actor claimed. He was not disinclined toward belief in such powers; some of the great actors and artists he had known seemed to draw from some intuitive source. But Zukor was a hardheaded businessman who acknowledged no such magic. In later conversations with Lasky he would often refer to Valentino as "The Power."

When Rudolph was informed that neither his request for Fitzmaurice nor shooting on location had been agreed to, he was incensed. Lasky explained that Fitzmaurice was not available and as for Spain, Zukor had turned down any additional strain on the budget. When Lasky informed him that director Fred Niblo would do the film, Rudolph's anger began to dissipate. Niblo, a fellow Italian whose original name had been Nobile, had just finished two films with Douglas Fairbanks, *The Mark of Zorro* and *The Three Musketeers*. As an ardent admirer of Fairbanks, Valentino felt that sharing his director certainly placed him high in filmdom's hierarchy.

As for Spain, Natacha had the answer. If they could not go there for locations, much of Spain could be imported. Without waiting for approval from the studio, she made arrangements to have authentic costumes made in Valentino's size in Spain. In addition, Spanish artifacts and the actual tools of the torreros were ordered: swords made from the finest Toledo steel, capes, muletas, picas and banderillas. When the studio accountants brought the bills for Valentino's purchases to Lasky's attention, he informed them to pay all charges.

Artists needed small acts of defiance for their egos. Zukor, too, took it philosophically. Successful business dealing required that each party feel that he had triumphed in some way.

Valentino began his psychic transformation into the soul of a matador. He took lessons to learn the various passes, and his dancer's legs and body made him an apt student. For the character of Juan Gallardo, Valentino drew from his own background the crudities and arrogance he believed to be that of a Spanish torero.

A full year before Stanislavski's Moscow Art Theater was to appear before the American public and a full decade before Lee Strasberg's Group Theater was to be formed, Valentino had begun to adopt some of the principles of "method" acting. Overly theatrical and undisciplined though he may have been, the roots of his performances lay in his ability to place himself within the role. He searched the character's background, emotions and motivations. Thus Valentino became the unschooled, naive Gallardo, not only in front of the camera, but off the set as well, in his behavior toward the director and studio executives and during his evening hours with Natacha.

Lasky had originally planned to have Bebe Daniels, one of the studio's stars, play the role of Doña Sol, the temptress who steals Gallardo away from his wife. And for the role of the wife, his first choice was the rising young star, May McAvoy. McAvoy was unavailable and her part was given to another of the many young adolescents around Hollywood who were playing adult roles, a sixteen-year-old named Lila Lee.

Daniels seemed to be ideally cast as Doña Sol. Ibañez had seen the heartless seductress as being a blond. However, upon meeting raven-haired, ex-Ziegfeld beauty Nita Naldi at a party where the two engaged in a highly charged argument, the author changed his mind. "You're the most vicious, cruel and beautiful woman I've ever met. You're the real Doña Sol!" he exclaimed. Nita, called Nitsy by her friends, was given the part.

After completing a memorable performance in *Blood and Sand*, Valentino began to look forward to untroubled days of happiness with Natacha. Now that there was a little time between pictures, he told her, perhaps they should get married. It seemed like a good idea at the time.

THE CONQUERING POWER

On the first of May, 1922, Valentino agreed to pay Jean Acker the sum of $12,000 for the release of all claims, present and in the future, said payment to be made in installments. To make the first payment, he borrowed $5,000 from the studio.

Twelve days later, Valentino and Natacha, accompanied by Nazimova, Paul Ivano and Doug Gerrard, spent the evening in Palm Springs. At a little after two the next afternoon, the group arrived at the home of Otto Moller, mayor of the little Mexican town of Mexicali, about one hundred and fifty miles south of Palm Springs. Mayor Moller was asked to perform a civil ceremony known as marriage. Despite the quick notice, Mayor Moller did the honors.

After the initial announcements of the marriage, the items in the daily papers took on an ominous tone. Judge John W. Summerfield of Los Angeles made the observation that the marriage, in his opinion, was invalid. It was his understanding that the divorce decree would not be finalized until a year had expired. If this were so, Rudolph had committed a bigamous act.

Jesse Lasky advised Valentino by telephone to make no comment to the press whatsoever. Rudy's immediate reaction was to run. Perhaps, he said to Lasky, a European tour might be apropos at this time. Lasky was firmly against such a move. Any appearance of flight would be detrimental, "After all, Rudy, your plea has got to be that you were not aware that an 'interlocutory decree' meant that the divorce had not been finalized." Lasky would meet with the studio's attorneys and call back.

Lasky called again to say that Will Hays, the recently appointed movie czar, was upset by the news and was considering suspension. Lasky suggested that Natacha and Rudolph return to L.A. for a meeting. There it was decided that Natacha should leave immediately to stay with her parents in upstate New York. Rudolph, accompanied by his attorney, W. I. Gilbert, would turn himself in to the district attorney. Rudolph did so and was placed in a cell with bail set for $10,000. It happened to be a Sunday, and banks were closed. No one was able to post a bond for his release.

The following day, Joseph Schenck, administrative head of United Artists, heard of Valentino's situation and offered to post an amount up to two hundred thousand dollars. By the time word got back to Schenck of the amount required, Valentino had been freed. June Mathis, director George Melford and Thomas Meighan had pooled their resources to come to the rescue. Most peculiar was Paramount's inactivity in this matter.

During the days that followed, it was discovered that Natacha Rambova was actually Winifred Shaunessy Hudnut, stepdaughter of Richard Hudnut, the multimillionaire cosmetic tycoon. This information, headlined in the press, made District Attorney Thomas Woodwine interested enough to take charge of the prosecution personally. At a time when Hollywood was fast gaining notoriety as a modern day Babylon, he was not unaware of the political hay that could be harvested.

Paramount's legal department, however, seasoned by recent scandals involving their top stars, had learned the adage of the football fields, "a good offense is the best defense." Accordingly, they had begun an investigation into the private life of Woodwine.

A few days before Valentino's trial was to begin, District Attorney Woodwine was charged by Miss Ida Wright Jones as having had intimate relations with her in hotels in the San Diego area. Miss Jones, a former employee in the DA's department, was willing to testify to the names of hotels and the dates on which these meetings took place. This unexpected turn of events curbed Woodwine's zeal.

The defense brought forth a parade of witnesses who testified that Valentino and Natacha had at no time been alone following their marriage. These included a maid serving the cottage occupied by the wedding party, a real estate broker, a neighbor and the owner of the cottage. Paul Ivano testified that the couple had occupied separate bedrooms. Doug Gerrard stated that he had occupied the same bedroom as Valentino during their Palm Springs stay. Nazimova, called as a witness for the state, did not appear. Heavily veiled, she had caught a train to New York the morning of her scheduled appearance and was found by reporters who met the train when it stopped in Chicago. The headlines of June 5 read, "NAZIMOVA SAYS SHE DIDN'T FLEE—Actress Denies She Left Hollywood to Escape Valentino Subpoena."

Readers of the L.A. *Examiner* the following day learned that Justice of the Peace J. Walter Hanby had dismissed the charge of bigamy against Valentino "for lack of sufficient evidence."

Following the trial, the relationship between Valentino and Paramount began to deteriorate. Paramount, having picked up the tab for all of the Spanish artifacts and costumes for *Blood and Sand,* and having made loans to Valentino for payments to Jean Acker, informed him that the cost for the legal services they had supplied would be withheld from his future salaries. Enraged, Valentino recalled indignities that the studio had caused him, the most recent of which was failing to come forth with the bigamy bail.

Rudolph was now convinced that the studio was not interested in him as a person but only as a salable commodity. The studio had no heart, only a giant ledger. Its compassion was dependent upon whether accounting entries were in black or red ink. In order to survive, he reasoned, he had to make outstanding movies. To make that type of picture, he required control over his stories, his writers, his directors and the principals in his casts.

Valentino and the studio were agreed in one respect. Another story had to be found for him. Natacha was thousands of miles away, and the actor was getting fidgety. Also, Lasky realized that publicity from the trial had brought public interest in Valentino to a peak. June Mathis had a story she believed to be perfect for him: An East Indian prince, adopted by a well-to-do American family as an infant and unaware of his true identity, grows up to become an outstanding student and athlete at Harvard. During this period he realizes that he has powers of clairvoyance. It was titled *The Young Rajah,* adapted from *Amos Judd,* a novel by John Ames Mitchell.

"Do me a favor, Junie. Show the story to Rudy but don't tell him I know anything about it," Lasky asked.

June informed Rudolph that she had a script that seemed right for him, one Lasky had been too busy to consider. She also gave him a copy for Natacha.

Valentino and Natacha had mixed reactions. Neither liked the story, although the clairvoyance theme was true to Rudy's psychic powers. Natacha, however, was intrigued by the possibility of designing exciting and innovative East Indian costumes for the film. Rudolph saw opportunities to show off his physique and display his athletic prowess—as Fairbanks did in his films.

Valentino dropped by Lasky's office to ask if the studio had come up with a story.

"It's been one of our major priorities, Rudy. We're looking but there's nothing around to match *The Sheik* or *Blood and Sand.*"

Rudolph mentioned that he had read Mathis' treatment of *Amos Judd.*

"Is that the one she calls *The Rajah?* It's got a lot of clairvoyance hokum in it and I don't think that audiences will go for it."

Lasky knew he had hit the bull's eye.

"Jesse," the actor rebutted, his temper rising, "it's not hokum! There are people who have a sixth sense about things. You've had premonitions about things before they happened, haven't you? I have, and millions of people believe it's possible. I know June does."

Lasky feigned capitulation. He offered Philip Rosen as director, indicating that Rosen was familiar with occult sciences. Actress Wanda Hawley (who had changed her name from Wanda Pettet for obvious reasons) was agreed upon as the female lead.

But if Lasky believed that his problems with Rudolph were over, he was to learn better. Valentino was used to leaning on Natacha for advice and encouragement. Since Natacha was still in New York, his day-to-day temperament was uneven. There were days when he was completely confident and cooperative. On other days, when uncertainties racked him, he would pace the floor, angry and argumentative, searching for the right interpretation.

The filming ground to an end with none of the participants satisfied. Rudolph, certain that he had been tricked by Lasky, thought the film weak and placed the blame on the studio. He announced plans to go to New York to see Natacha. With Paramount paying expenses, he would make a personal appearance in New York City at the premiere of *Blood and Sand*.

En route, he apparently changed his mind. When the train arrived in New York, Rudolph, instead of going to the Waldorf where the studio had reserved a suite for him, caught the first train out for Albany. There he was met by limousine and taken to Foxlair, home of the Richard Hudnuts.

The premiere of *Blood and Sand*—sans a personal appearance by its star—proved that Paramount could come up with a success to match *The Sheik*. Reviewers lavished praise on Valentino's portrayal of Juan Gallardo, the peasant boy who becomes Spain's greatest bullfighter and after an affair with a selfish siren is gored by a bull to die in the arms of his faithful wife.

Paramount's joy was tempered by Rudolph's behavior. There were no phones in Foxlair, and letters and wires to Valentino went unanswered. Finally, word from Valentino arrived. It was a letter, not from the actor himself, but from lawyers he had appointed in New York. Paramount had been put on notice that Mr. Valentino sought release from his contract and trusted this might be done as amicably as possible.

Paramount's reply was firm and to the point. They had no intention of releasing the actor from his contract and, if necessary, would take the matter to court. Valentino's answer was a request that the studio refrain from sending him any further salary since he no longer considered himself employed by them.

In mid-September, Paramount filed for an injunction to prevent Valentino from contracting himself to anyone else "for pictures or on the 'speaking stage' " since these appearances were still under an existing valid contract that would not expire until February 7, 1924. Documents that followed stated that a picture for Valentino titled *The Spanish Cavalier* had been scheduled for production at the start of September and that losses incurred, due to the absence of its principal actor, totalled $30,000 to date.

Valentino's counter-complaint stated that it was Paramount who had originally breached the contract by its substitution of two women in the leading roles of *Blood and Sand*—Nita Naldi and Lila Lee for Bebe Daniels and May McAvoy—which had served to damage his standing; the refusal of the studio to share the cost of answering his fan mail, which ran over a thousand letters weekly; inadequate dressing room facilities; and a charge that since his trip to New York, he had been under constant surveillance by private detectives in the employ of Paramount, the purpose of which could only be to catch him in illicit cohabitation with Natacha Rambova.

In order to stay in close communication with his legal counsel, Rudolph left Foxlair to take a suite at the Hotel des Artistes on West 67th Street which he shared with Frank Menillo, an old friend. Natacha and her aunt, Mrs. Teresa Werner, also left the country estate and found an apartment on the same street.

Natacha, while she shared Rudolph's dislike of the studio and his need for control over his pictures, did not completely approve of his actions. She began to view him more and more as a child, governed by impulse.

But Rudolph believed in a divinity somewhere that watches over children strayed. He was confident that though he had cut himself off from his only source of income, something, or someone, would take care of him.

And, so it happened. Frank Joseph Godsol was hardly a saint, but for Rudolph and Natacha his head bore a halo. Godsol, an American who had become a French citizen, had made a fortune during the war buying American munitions and selling them to France. Rudolph had met him through Sam Goldwyn who had brought Godsol and his millions into the film industry. The "Sun God," as Rudolph would occasionally call him, making a play on his name, not only provided the actor with living expenses but also took care of the billings from his New York attorney. For this, Godsol asked only that he be repaid when Valentino had resolved his situation and was again earning money.

With long hours at their disposal, Rudolph and Natacha became more and more involved in spiritualism, stimulated by the death of the mother of one of Natacha's friends. Shortly after the older lady had expired, the daughter began hearing mysterious rapping sounds which she accepted as messages from her mother. The rappings were soon followed by messages received from the "other side" through automatic writing. One message was directed to Rudolph, and Natacha's friend forwarded it as transcribed. It came from Rudolph's mother, Gabriella. Within it were references to incidents in Rudolph's childhood that—according to the amazed actor—no one else in the States knew anything about. This so intrigued the two of them that they began having regular meetings at Natacha's apartment. Here they both got involved in automatic writing although Rudolph, by far, was the more receptive.

At these meetings they first became communicants with Meselope, an ancient Egyptian, and Black Feather, an Indian. Black Feather brought prophesies; Meselope, spiritual guidance.

According to Black Feather, Paramount's injunction against Rudolph would be modified in his favor. The spirit of the Indian guide also informed them that the couple would be making a long trip that would take them to many cities, and that they would soon meet a man who would become Rudolph's new business manager.

In October, *The Young Rajah* was premiered in New York to poor reviews. Despite the lukewarm notices, the public—mostly women—filled the theaters, bearing out Lasky's prognostications. Valentino's stature as a star, whose pictures the public would flock to see regardless of the quality, had been proven.

The Young Rajah became a bone of contention between Valentino and Paramount. The studio claimed that the actor had been responsible for the choice of the weak story; this was what would happen if Valentino were given artistic control. Valentino, aware of Lasky's ploy from his conversations with June Mathis, rebutted that the picture was Paramount's idea and that he had been tricked into making it.

Seeking to win the actor back before animosities deepened, the studio—now fully aware that Valentino's popularity superceded weak stories—offered to raise the actor's salary to $7,000 a week. When Valentino's attorneys relayed this offer to their client, the actor was sorely tempted. The money was far more than he had hoped to get, although phenomenal salaries were being paid at the time. Gloria Swanson was earning close to $750,000 a year. But then, he reasoned, money had not been the object of his rebellion and because of that, he turned it down. What he truly wanted had not been offered: artistic control of his pictures.

In an "Open Letter to the American Public," published in *Photoplay,* January 1923, Valentino presented his case to the multitudes. He announced that his primary desire had never been monetary but "to make real photoplays instead of cut-and-dried program features that can be hacked and compressed into a given number of feet of film." "Art," he concluded, "cannot be measured by inches."

When Valentino refused its salary offer, Paramount decided that the battle was a stalemate. To capitalize on the public's demand for movies of the Great Lover, they reissued some of his earlier films. Other studios went into their warehouses to retrieve films gathering dust. New opening titles were made, announcing the star of the film as Rudolph Valentino—despite the minor role he played—and put back into distribution. *The Married Virgin* was re-released as *Frivolous Wives;* *An Adventuress* became *Isle of Love;* and, *A Rogue's Romance,* which contained a dance sequence featuring Valentino, was re-edited with portions of the dance duplicated and spliced back into the film to extend the sequence several times its original length.

Among the hundreds of thousands who read Valentino's impassioned presentation of his case in *Photoplay* was a public relations man named S. George Ullman. Ullman found himself intrigued by the plight of Valentino. Here was a young man, twenty-seven years old, who at the height of his fame was being denied the right to make motion pictures or act on the stage. Surely, he thought to himself, there must be something that this man, adulated by millions of women, could do to capitalize on his fame. The thought came to him of producing some sort of booklet featuring the star in photographs from his many pictures. A booklet of this type—bearing an autographed picture of the star on the cover—would certainly sell into the millions. Ullman decided to see as many of the Valentino re-releases as possible.

It was while watching Valentino dance in *The Four Horsemen* that inspiration came. The man was a marvelous dancer and, according to what he had read, the girl whom he loved was also a former dancer. Why not a dance tour sponsored by one of his clients? When he came to the Mineralava Beauty Clay company on his client list, he knew he had something. Valentino's appeal was primarily to women and the Mineralava company had been looking for a way to promote their product to the American women. He contacted the company and they were interested: How much would it cost? Ullman knew that he could not go under the amount Paramount had offered. Seven thousand a week plus expenses, he said. The executives of Mineralava agreed to those terms. Next, he had to sell the idea to Valentino.

When Ullman appeared with his proposition, Valentino was quite receptive. He had neither worked nor received income for almost ten months. The couple signed for the tour.

There was one important thing that had to be attended to. On March 14, with Michael Romano, assistant District Attorney of Chicago, and Aunt Teresa as witnesses, Rudolph Valentino and Natacha Rambova had their second marriage ceremony in Crown Point, Indiana.

The tour, which began in Omaha, Nebraska, was conducted in style. Ullman had engaged a private railroad car for the couple along with a chef and a steward. The luxurious accommodations were soon to be appreciated, for the tour of one-nighters proved to be a grueling one. At times, petty incidents triggered arguments, but Ullman developed a comfortable closeness with the newlywed Valentinos. In San Antonio, Texas, Rudolph asked Ullman if he would like a full-time job as his business manager. Ullman refused. Pressed for a reason, he explained that while he enjoyed the couple very much, it would be a risky move for him to make. "Look, Rudy, I've been going over your debts and you're in hock over $50,000. Right now you can afford me because of the seven grand a week you're making, but what happens after the tour? What will Paramount let you go into?"

Rudolph smiled. "Have confidence in me, George," he said.

"I do," Ullman replied. "But the way you and your Mrs. throw away money is really frightening."

"George, that's why we need a business manager."

Ullman promised he would give it more thought. Ten weeks later when the tour was nearing its end, Ullman brought the matter up again. "If the offer's still open, I'll take it," he said.

Rudolph's smile was almost cocky as he said, "I knew you would."

"How come you were so damn sure?"

"George, you have to remember. I have a friend who tells me these things."

At first Ullman thought that Rudy was referring to Natacha, but then he remembered the couple sitting together in the lounge of their private car communicating with the spirits. Black Feather! Damn, he thought, if they can communicate with a dead Indian who can predict the future, what do they need me for?

Ullman insisted on complete control over all of Rudolph's business dealings; Natacha would have no say whatsoever. This agreed upon, he discharged Valentino's New York attorney, paying a $48,000 fee that was due. He also paid back $15,000 to Godsol and Joseph Schenck, who had been providing the Valentinos with living expenses prior to the Mineralava tour. He hired attorney Max D. Steuer to begin working on the Paramount situation and put the actor and his wife on a strict budget. The dance tour had brought the Valentinos $119,000. By the time Ullman had finished settling debts, there was little left.

Then, with Max Steuer by his side, he went to a meeting called by Adolph Zukor. When they walked into the New York offices of the trim little emperor of Paramount, they found him in the company of a heavy-set, moonfaced man who was introduced as J. D. Williams, a pioneer movie exhibitor who was planning to become an independent producer.

Zukor, whose doleful eyes masked the keenest mind in the industry, had conceived a masterful plan. He offered to advance the producer's percentage of box office receipts toward production costs of films to be made by Williams' new firm, Ritz-Carlton Pictures, in exchange for exclusive distribution rights. As for Valentino, he would be given the artistic control he wanted and a weekly salary of $7,500 for which he would be committed for only two more pictures. Thereafter, his contract would be assigned to Ritz-Carlton.

The deal would put Williams in business with a top star; give Valentino all he wanted; and after two films, free Paramount of all production headaches with its temperamental actor while it retained exclusive distribution rights to all of his films.

Rudolph considered it a triumph—which it was for all concerned. The new contract gave him the right of veto over stories, directors, co-stars and writers. Fur-

ther, it gave Natacha control over the artistic aspects of
his films. The $7,500 a week would become effective
once his signature was affixed to the contract.

Rudolph signed. He hugged Ullman, kissing him on
the cheek. He put his arm around Max Steuer as Natacha brought forth a bottle of champagne. Now he
had everything he and Natacha had wanted—and a
star's salary as well.

With their long battle with the studio ended, the
Valentinos boarded the *Aquitania* for a much needed
vacation—with pay. They were bound for Europe
where they would relax at the Hudnut villa in Juan les
Pins; visit London and Paris; and then drive into Italy
to spend time with Rudolph's brother and sister—his
first visit to his homeland since leaving it ten years
earlier.

PART TWO

"Ten years ago I came to America poor, friendless, unknown and penniless. I didn't know what I was going to do. I didn't know what was to become of me. No one met me when I landed at the pier. No one even knew I was coming, and if they had known, it wouldn't have made the least difference in the world to a living soul ...

"I shall never go home, I said to myself, until I can go home SOMEBODY!

"The mere thought, the poor, thin, fruitless hope of such a thing thrilled me to the very core. To have left, as I left, poor and unknown, a Nobody. To go back ... rich, famous, successful ... What a desire! What a dream!"

—Rudolph Valentino
(from his diary)

SEPTEMBER 17, 1923

At the corner he braked the big touring car and waved for the last time at the group in the courtyard. He could see them wave back—Alberto, Ada, Maria, and his little nephew, Jean—but in the half-light of dawn he could no longer make out their faces. *"Ciao,* dear ones," he said so softly that only the woman beside him heard. He let out the clutch a little too rapidly and the Voisin leapt forward into the narrow, uneven cobblestone street that led to the main road.

Natacha must surely be back at Chateau les Pins by now. Asleep in the Louis XVI fourposter, her hair tousled and dark against the white down pillow. Only when she was asleep did she appear unguarded, and relaxed.

It was in Rome that she announced she would go no further: "I'm black and blue from bouncing on those hideous roads. My lungs are coated with half the dust of Italy and my nerves are raw from your reckless driving"—all delivered in that icy, controlled tone he had learned not to contradict. Gently, he'd placed his arms around her shoulders and insisted that she return to her parents' chateau in southern France where she could rest. What else was there to do?

The road before him swept into a wide curve. He was headed toward his birthplace. Turning to the woman beside him, he shouted above the roar of the Voisin's engine, "Good-bye, Campobasso! Hello, Castellaneta!"

She could have been his mother. Though in her mid-fifties she still looked young and, despite her

85

sharp features, attractive. She smiled at the young man at the wheel. "Castellaneta or bust!" she said.

Who could ask for a better traveling companion than Mrs. Teresa Werner, the sister of his wife's mother? Here was a woman who never became ruffled, never complained. When the Voisin required hand-cranking to start it, she knew exactly when to retard the spark and how far the manual choke had to be extended. When the right front tire had been punctured, it was Aunt Teresa who had pitched in—while Natacha sought a shady spot to sit. Yes, a truly remarkable woman!

His older brother's refusal to join them had been a disappointment. At first, it had been polite: "Rodolfo, you're on a holiday and have time to spend looking for your childhood. As you can see, I must work so that my family may eat."

Certain that Alberto only needed further coaxing, Rudy had repeated the invitations during the week they'd spent in Campobasso. Finally Alberto's patience gave out. "To see what? An old house where I've not lived for twenty years? People I've forgotten as they've forgotten me? An old village with nothing but dirt, stones and poverty? Keep your childhood fantasies, Rodolfo! I cannot afford them!"

Initially, Maria, the young sister, had agreed to go with Rodolfo to Castellaneta. But that had been in Milan when she had been caught in the excitement of their reunion. In the days that followed—the long trip to Rome with stops in Pisa to see the Leaning Tower, and to Florence to visit the museums and the Ponte Vecchio shops—she had become aware of how vast the gulf was that separated them. Ten years earlier, a cocky, unsophisticated youth—with whom she had shared so many childhood secrets—had boarded a boat in Taranto, and now this polished, confident stranger with shaped eyebrows and slicked-back hair had returned.

When Natacha decided to return to France, Maria had seen the hurt in her brother's face and shared the shame he must have felt. What self-respecting Italian man would accept such treatment from his wife? A silence came upon them and she was relieved to arrive in Campobasso. She threw herself at Alberto, embraced Ada, his wife, and made an extraordinary fuss over their baby son, Jean. Later—before informing Rodolfo—she confided to Ada her decision not to go to Castellaneta. The wife agreed. "If Rodolfo's wife did not choose to stay with her husband, why should you force yourself to make such an arduous trip."

And so it was that there were but two occupants in the big touring car.

South of Andria—on a hill from where the Adriatic could be seen, shimmering along the horizon—Rudolph pulled the car to a stop amidst a patch of trees. Here the two lunched on bread baked by Alberto's wife, goat cheese, sausages, and red wine.

Afterward, Rudolph lay back on the blanket and quickly fell asleep. Teresa looked down at the man dozing beside her. How peaceful he looked now—so much like an overgrown child. She reached over and—ever so gently, lest she might awaken him—brushed back strands of hair that had fallen across his forehead. Natacha should be here; strong-willed, high-strung, fiercely stubborn Natacha should watch him as he slept —those hooded, romantic eyes now closed so peacefully. Natacha should be the one looking down on him lovingly. Stroking cheeks browned by the sun; and with her fingers, tracing the contours of his lips.

The young man stirred awake. He was immediately apologetic. "I'm sorry, Aunt Teresa. I must have fallen asleep. We must go."

The roar of the Voisin's engine thundered again. The late summer's dust, mixed with the exhaust, swirled like a cloud behind the car as it once more bounced along the torturous road.

On the other side of Gioia del Colle the road forked and he instinctively turned into the smaller, less traversed one that led to the right. A feeling of deja vu gripped him. He had come this way with his father? Or was it that he had wandered alone along these rocky hillsides, probing into caves that pockmarked this countryside. In one especially large cavern he had discovered the remains of an ancient church. Always, during

these wanderings, he would find a road or a path that
would eventually lead him home.

Then a strange, ominous foreboding tightened his
stomach. Was Black Feather, his spiritual Indian guide,
sending him a warning? Neither Natacha, Alberto, nor
Maria had joined him. Had they been forewarned? Was
something preordained awaiting the arrival of Teresa and himself and none other? Memories, long re-
pressed but loosened by the familiarity of the land
around him, came forth in a torrent abounding with
questions. Hadn't he always been the favored child of
his mother, cuddled and kissed because of his good
looks? Why then had he sought the comfort of his
fantasies in the darkness of caves? Was this not because
he had been a recalcitrant, requiring the severe discipline of his father and uncles? The tightness in his
stomach became more intense.

In the distance, the houses of Castellaneta came
into view. Small bleached limestone rectangles clustered
atop a hill that suddenly dropped off into a stony
canyon on the far side. He braked sharply in the village square; it was smaller than he'd expected. The dust
rose, glistening in the late afternoon sun. Turning the
engine off, he heard the angry barking of dogs. Within
seconds, a dog dashed into the square followed by a
young boy. The boy and dog stopped a safe distance
away and studied the intruders.

Rudolph helped the older woman out of the car and
led her to a white house on a corner. He looked at it,
memories flooding back. He saw his bedroom. He remembered how the morning sun would come into the
windows. He opened the hood of his camera and
checked the settings. "Stand over there, Aunt Teresa,"
he said. "We must have pictures to show the others."

Teresa moved toward the doorway, adjusting her hat.
As she faced the camera she saw that the square was
gradually filling with people. Men in worn, baggy
clothes moved toward the big touring car. Two young
boys clambered on the high running board to examine
the instrument panel. Short, stout women in drab, shape-
less dresses—some with aprons tied at midriff—clustered in little groups, gesticulating. Rudolph seemed

unaware of the spectators. He held the camera at waist-level, squinted into the hood and snapped the shutter.

"Rudy, I think we have an audience."

The young man turned, saw the people and smiled. He aimed the camera toward the Voisin and those surrounding it. Murmurs of protest greeted this action. Men who had been watching almost motionless quickly scurried out of the camera's aim. From the large church facing the square, a black-robed priest emerged and hurried toward the strange intruder.

"*Buona sera,* Father," Rudolph said loudly. "Do you remember me? I am Guglielmi. The son, Rodolfo. My father cared for the animals here. We lived in this house."

"Yes, yes. Guglielmi the *veterinario.* I remember— but not well. It has been at least twenty years, yes?" His eyes scrutinized the elegant automobile and turned back to examine the tailored clothing the young man wore. "Now you've returned wealthy to this poor village. As you can see, the church is very old and in need of repair."

The crowd, silent and strangely hostile, moved in and encircled the priest, the newcomers and the car. The young man's poised confidence, so much a part of his being, seemed to dissipate slowly as he stood in the village square of his youth. He was confronted by the menacing figure of a priest, in whose presence he always felt guilt. Surrounding him were poor villagers. There was not a smile or a sign of recognition from any of them. Rudolph reached into his pocket and brought forth a handful of liras. Several he handed to the priest. "A donation for your church, Father." One bill fluttered to the ground. Instantly, a young boy scooped it up and disappeared into a side street.

"*Signore,* you have brought money for me, too?" It was an old woman, harsh and whining.

Others took up the cry. The crowd pressed forward. Open palms were extended. Rudolph was bewildered. He thrust Teresa toward the car and the two climbed aboard. He turned the key and pressed the self-starter. The engine caught immediately and the sound of it thundering and reverberating within the square immobilized the people momentarily, but the arms remained outstretched. Rudolph threw the handful of bills in the air. While they still fluttered to the ground, men, women and children began scrambling for them. Rudolph put the car into gear and drove away.

A weather-hardened chunk of goat dung was hurled through the window. It struck the inside of the windshield and landed on the seat between the driver and his companion. Rudolph picked up the dung and held it for a moment. "Money, money, money, *this* is money," he said. Then he tossed it away.

The sun disappeared behind the hills. The long, tiring day was near its end. Rudolph narrowed his eyes. Soon they would be in Taranto. There would be a hot bath, delicious *zuppa di pesce*, good wine and music. There were movie houses in Taranto. Perhaps someone there might know his name.

Yes, in Taranto it would be better.

THE FALCON AND THE EAGLE

Ten years before an unsmiling eighteen-year-old had pressed against the railing of the *SS Cleveland* to stare through narrowed eyes as the giant outline of the Lady of Liberty came into view. Now, as the *Belgenland* glided slowly past Bedloe's Island toward a city turned friendly, the same young man entered the harbor again—this time dressed in the best from Savile Row, and accompanied by a lovely woman who was his wife. Rodolfo Guglielmi may have been frightened. Rudolph Valentino was not.

Ullman was there to meet them at the docks. After their trunks—filled with purchases made in London, Paris and Rome—had cleared customs, they took a cab to the Ritz-Carlton Hotel where Ullman had reserved a luxurious suite.

"How appropriate," Natacha said as she gathered her two Pekinese up into her arms and stepped out on the red runner that led from the entrance of the hotel to the curbing. "It's quite right that we should stay at the Ritz-Carlton upon our return."

Ullman laughed. "I thought you might like it as an omen of good things to come. I'm sure Jaydee will be pleased."

On the late afternoon of the next day, the Valentinos met with Ullman and Max Steuer to make a decision on the various stories that Paramount had optioned for Rudolph's next picture. The choice narrowed down to two: *Captain Blood,* a swashbuckling sea adventure to be adapted from the best-selling novel by Rafael Sabatini; and *Monsieur Beaucaire,* an early Booth Tarkington novel about the adventures of a French prince traveling through England during the time of Louis XVI.

Rudolph, who had been so moved by *The Sea Hawk,* an earlier Sabatini novel, that he longed to play the leading character on the screen, favored *Captain Blood.* He wanted an opportunity to prove that his athletic abilities and his swordsmanship were as good as Douglas Fairbanks'.

Natacha, however, was insistent on *Monsieur Beaucaire.* Natacha cooly cited her points: "Why try to compete with Fairbanks when you have your own image, Rudy? Women see you as an elegant, dashing gentleman with courtly manners. *Captain Blood* is all action and fighting while *Beaucaire* will show off the sensitivity of your acting. And, we can include fencing scenes and a dressing scene to show off your physique."

Blood offered few challenges to a costume or set designer: *Beaucaire,* on the other hand, would be a veritable *tour de force.*

Rudolph did not give in readily, but the decision, for all practical purposes, had been made. Ullman handled his business affairs; Steuer was his legal counsel; and Natacha had taken over his personal life and creative decisions.

Natacha, given "artistic control" by the new contract, immediately assumed a position comparable to a working producer. With the aid of three assistants, she made her presence known throughout the Astoria lot. She supervised the costume designer, the scenic designer, the makeup supervisor, the interiors designer and, on the set, she got involved with the director and cameraman. Iron-willed, demanding perfection regardless of cost, she created tumult wherever she went. At her insistence, sixty costumes were created in Paris according to designs researched for their authenticity by experts and sketched by the top French illustrator of the day. Lavish sets were constructed and decorated with priceless antiques. The cost of producing *Monsieur Beaucaire* would be second to none.

When *Beaucaire* opened at the Mark Strand theater in New York, Natacha's work was rewarded with high praise. *The New York Times* reported: "Gorgeous is a word we invariably dodge, but this pictorial effort is thoroughly deserving of such an adjective, as never before have such wondrous settings or beautiful costumes been seen in a photoplay."

As for the star, *Photoplay* capsuled the faults: "Rudy plays the part of a prince of France, and, except for one or two situations in which he puts over rattling good sword fights, the old spark disappears. He doesn't look dangerous to women.

"The fact of the matter is that they like their Rudy a little wicked. He had what is known in pictures as 'menace' to a higher degree than any other actor on the screen. In *Beaucaire* he has as much of this quality as Charlie Chaplin."

Natacha's victory was complete. Not only had she married the man who filled the fantasies of palpitating women the world over, but she had made of him her personal mannequin. She had dressed him in outrageous silks, satin and laces; bewigged and powdered him; and upon his cheek affixed a tiny, heart-shaped "valentine," a beauty mark. Not only tamed the savage sheik; erased every vestige of that menacing primitive, and in doing so she had made him second to her "wondrous" sets and "gorgeous" costumes.

The final review, the one all studios live by, was yet to come—from the accounting department. When it arrived, the bottom line indicated: *Beaucaire* was not only a fop; it was also a flop.

The *Monsieur Beaucaire* experience soured Adolph Zukor on the Valentinos. Where once he had only a temperamental, often irrational, actor to deal with, now there was a stubborn, demanding woman in tandem.

Anxious to shed the studio of these two "Powers" as quickly as possible, especially since Rudolph's salary continued whether he was working or not, Zukor ordered the story department to provide the two with as many properties as the studio had options on. Of these, Natacha liked Rex Beach's novel, *Rope's End*. For the screen, the story was retitled, *The Sainted Devil*.

When it came to the leading lady, Natacha made a strong stand. She insisted on Nita Naldi. Since the fall in popularity of the original "vamp," Theda Bara, Nitsy Naldi had become the screen's leading temptress. Natacha reasoned that the public would enjoy seeing her paired with Rudy once again as the "other woman." A promising young starlet, Helen D'Algy, was cast as Rudolph's wife.

Joseph Henabery, the director, was prepared to face the worst on the set from an opinionated Natacha. Surprisingly, he ran into few problems. Natacha was already thinking beyond this last film for Paramount. She was personally writing a scenario to be called *The Hooded Falcon*. Meanwhile, on the set, Valentino was glorying in a role that permitted him, for the first time, to sully his flawless screen image by showing uncontrolled rage, deep despondency and drunkenness.

With their final picture for Paramount in the can, Natacha and Rudolph met with Jaydee Williams in the new offices of Ritz-Carlton Pictures in New York. It was to be the most stimulating, and certainly the most enjoyable meeting they would have with their new employer. Williams listened with unrestrained delight as his newly-acquired talents—the superstar lover and his brilliant, artistic wife—outlined the story of *The Hooded Falcon*. They could have sold Williams a remake of *Intolerance*.

Williams agreed to a preliminary budget of forty thousand to be used toward further research. With this generous vote of confidence, the Valentinos left for Spain to engage in a buying spree. Inside of a month the preliminary budget had been exceeded by twice the amount. Crates of costumes, tapestries, antique weapons, etchings, armor, horse saddles and miscellaneous artifacts began to arrive marked: "The Hooded Falcon Co., care of Ritz-Carlton Pictures."

The couple then moved on to Paris where Natacha spent her days making sketches of medieval costumes from paintings in the Louvre. Rudolph, in his new Voisin tourer, tested its power with drives around the countryside. He also visited the Hotel des Invalides where he studied the heraldic costumes and weapons on display.

In Paris, they ran into Nita Naldi, who was immediately offered a part in the new movie and joined the couple on their research jaunts into the countryside. Meanwhile, Valentino began to experiment with a full beard—which Natacha approved as being ideal for his portrayal of a Moor.

When telegrams from Ullman convinced them that Williams' patience was beginning to wear thin, the trio returned to New York. Among those whom the beard impressed was Harry Reichenbach, Rudolph's friend from his days as a bit player. Reichenbach, still working as a publicist for Paramount, had been assigned the task of publicizing *The Sainted Devil,* now being readied for a New York premiere.

First, he saw to it that the Great Lover's new facial adornment was given national coverage. Noting that the Master Barbers Association was holding its annual convention in Chicago, he sent news clippings and pictures of the bearded Valentino to the president of the association with a carefully worded letter that spoke of the dark days that might lay ahead for the tonsorial profession. The Great Lover was growing a beard. What would this do to the barbers of the nation?

A resolution was passed on the floor of the convention: Either Rudolph Valentino would shave his beard, or he would suffer a boycott of all his films by barbers, their wives, families and friends! While the humor of this did not escape Valentino, he was forced to succumb and a publicity photograph of a barber attacking his facial foliage made the national newspapers.

Meanwhile, the bills from the research trip were arriving in batches. Williams called June Mathis in Hollywood, where she was trying to bring Natacha's unrelated scenes together into a cohesive story. The job seemed hopeless. Williams asked if it would help if Natacha was present for consultation. Mathis was not eager to have Natacha looking over her shoulder, but she decided that it might help.

Aware that Valentino's contract called for $7,500 a week whether he was working or not, Williams purchased screen rights to a Broadway play that had been enjoying a long run, *Cobra.* He met with the Valentinos and presented his problem. The delays and preproduction costs on *The Hooded Falcon* had caused the financial backers in Ritz-Carlton to become increasingly unhappy. It was important to the survival of the new company that the Valentinos work on *Cobra* prior to *The Hooded Falcon*.

Natacha eyed Williams with cold suspicion. "We had talked about filming many of the scenes for 'The Hooded Falcon' in Spain, with the understanding that the budget for the film would be a million dollars. Have these plans been changed?"

Williams nodded. *The Sainted Devil* had just opened to weak reviews. This, coupled with the reports about *Beaucaire,* had caused his backers to retrench. Location work in Spain would have to be forgotten, since the budget was slashed in half. *Cobra* would be filmed in Hollywood with production to begin as quickly as possible. Natacha would make herself available to June Mathis so that the *Falcon* scenario could be completed.

Natacha replied that if the *Falcon*'s budget was slashed in half, it needed her full attention. The reduced budget would necessitate vast changes in sets and costumes. "Besides," she added, *"Cobra* is a contemporary play, and there's little I can contribute to it."

Their relationship with Williams severely strained, the Valentinos boarded a train to return to Hollywood. They had been gone two years.

To celebrate their return to the film capital, they hosted a lavish party at the Ambassador Hotel, inviting several hundred notables from the film colony and the community at large. Among the top stars at this gala affair were Charles Chaplin with his young love, Lita Grey, Doug Fairbanks and Mary Pickford, Harold Lloyd, Marion Davies, Clara Bow, Mae Murray, John Gilbert, John Barrymore and Tom Mix.

Despite the success of their affair, it was the last big party that the Valetinos would host. Williams' change in attitude, so evident in their last meeting, was but a prelude to their problems.

Among these was the break-up of their long friendship with June Mathis. June had written a number of original scenes and Natacha saw these as injurious to the way she visualized the story. Natacha began a complete rewrite.

Natacha telephoned Williams informing him that she was dissatisfied with June's work and that she was revising the scenario personally. When June heard about the situation from Williams, she was indignant. When Natacha called her a week later, June refused to discuss the matter.

Natacha's frustrations in piecing together a cohesive scenario for *The Hooded Falcon* soon colored other parts of her life. Unable to resolve a problem in the script, she would drive to the set of *Cobra* and invariably disrupt the shooting with her insistence on changes. The Hollywood she once found so exciting she now referred to as being little more than sham and more sham. She refused to entertain and became annoyed when Rudolph's friends came over to visit.

The house no longer suited her. There was a time when happiness was a Christmas tree, a chair in the living room, and a dog in a stocking. Now, the house was filled with furniture, expensive antiques and pets, but happiness was gone. Natacha never lost an opportunity to tell Rudolph that the house was much too small for a star of his magnitude.

Tempers collided and sparks flew. Little spats became heated arguments to be followed by long silences. Each became more involved in activities that excluded the other. Natacha drove into the countryside, presumably to find locations for *The Hooded Falcon*. Rudolph worked on his car. He met his friends away from home.

Yet there were days when the two were close and loving. Christmas came, and she gave him a slave bracelet—made to her design at Tiffany's. He gave her a wristwatch set into a moonstone and encrusted with diamonds. Then, too, there was their common love of animals. She had ten Pekinese dogs that were always scampering underfoot, and he had his Great Danes, German Shepherds, and horses. They had an aviary built close to the house and stocked with small birds, and a pond filled with carp. For the new movie, Rudy

ordered trained falcons from Europe. Falcons had always fascinated them.

In hopes of appeasing Natacha and saving his faltering
marriage, Rudolph began a search for a new house. In
due time one was found. It was like a Mediterranean
villa, surrounded by stately cypresses, built atop a knoll
of a hill that looked over Beverly Hills from Beverly
Glen Road. The lot spanned eight acres and the
grounds were beautifully landscaped. Adjoining the
house was a four-car garage, the second level of which
had been made into a six-room servants' quarters.
Looking southwest from the windows—between the
trees that climbed up the steep hillside—he could see
the shimmer in the distance that was the Pacific Ocean.
It was perfect. In this house, so remote and serene,
they would find happiness again.

While the new house was being redecorated, Rudolph visited it often to make certain that the work was
being done to the perfection he demanded. One day
he took along a falcon, setting it free to ride the winds
before returning to his wrist. It was then that he recalled the Hudnuts' estate: Foxlair. This house, too,
should have a name. It would be called Falcon's Lair.
Natacha would like that.

Shooting on *Cobra* was completed and a rough print
was rushed to J. D. Williams who immediately
screened it for those who had invested money into Ritz-
Carlton Pictures. After an hour and twenty minutes the
overhead lights were turned up to reveal grim-faced
men. There was no enthusiasm. Later that afternoon a
call was made to George Ullman; he was to notify the
Valentinos that with the release of *Cobra* the company
known as Ritz-Carlton Pictures was being dissolved. All
contracts and committments were cancelled forthwith.

It meant the certain demise of *The Hooded Falcon*.
A dream that was one of the last remaining ties between the Valentinos had been shattered.

When the news of the dissolution of Ritz-Carlton became public, it was Joseph Schenck who again appeared
on the scene as if mounted on a white charger. In a
meeting with Ullman, he offered Valentino a contract

with United Artists at a salary of $10,000 per week—a substantial amount for an actor whose last few pictures had done poorly.

There was one very interesting clause in the contract: Natacha Rambova Valentino was to have no say in any of her husband's films. Further, her presence on the set of her husband's films would not be welcomed.

Natacha's reaction was cold fury, aimed not at Schenck, but at her husband: what sort of man would permit his wife to be so grossly maligned? Had it not been for her guidance, he might still be working for a pittance with Paramount. He would never have been a star without her. Angered, defiant, Rudolph signed the contract that eliminated his wife from further participation in his career.

The schism between them became irreparable.

To welcome the Great Lover to its folds, United Artists gave a gala dinner at the Roosevelt Hotel in New York. Natacha, poised and smiling, successfully camouflaged her anger and bitterness. Standing next to her husband, her arm locked with his, she said, "Mr. Schenck is such a wonderful man."

The first movie United Artists readied for Valentino was titled *The Eagle,* adapted from Pushkin's novel, *Dobrovsky.* Vilma Banky, the beautiful blond Hungarian actress, would be his leading lady.

Meanwhile, Ullman came up with a brilliant idea. Observing Natacha's increasing unhappiness and the effect it was having on Valentino, he suggested that she be given the opportunity to make her own film. Rudolph took the idea to Natacha and her response was enthusiastic. She wanted to make a satiric commentary on the ridiculous ends to which women went in order to make themselves attractive for men. She decided to call her opus, *What Price Beauty?,* an obvious take-off on the male-oriented war movie, *What Price Glory?*

To produce the film, a new corporation was created, funded by the earnings of the star, The Rudolph Valentino Production Company.

Natacha quickly immersed herself in the rigors of producing and directing her film. Banned from involvement in her husband's career, she made it known that no one from United Artists would be welcome in her home.

What Price Beauty?, expeditiously confined to indoor stages and efficiently produced, was quickly completed. Nita Naldi headed the cast which included Myrna Loy in a minor role. The preview screening in Pasadena was not promising. Natacha decided to market the film in New York.

Aware that a break-up was imminent, the Hollywood press corps was out in full force when Rudolph accompanied his producer-wife to her train. If animosity existed, the couple concealed it well. Arms around each other, they denied all rumors about marital problems. They staged and restaged embraces and kisses.

Natacha's attempts to sell the film in New York were futile, aside from a few scattered showings.

Rudolph's behaviour began to take a suicidal bent. Oblivious to the arguments of director Clarence Brown, he shunned the use of stunt men for dangerous scenes and more than once suffered injuries. Off the set, his reckless driving was maniacal. He was arrested for speeding in Santa Monica. He ran the Voisin into a telephone pole on Western Avenue. He was a man torn with inner wounds, recklessly challenging fate.

He began to be seen at major social functions that he and Natacha had previously shunned. His companion at these parties was his *Eagle* leading lady, Vilma Banky, triggering many items in the columns. Among the many adoring eyes that flirted with his at these affairs, one pair belonged to Pola Negri. It had come to be known that whatever Pola wants, Pola gets.

Their meeting took place at Marion Davies' spectacular mansion in Santa Monica. Valentino arrived with Vilma. He was wearing the Cossack costume from *The Eagle,* but he was upstaged by a bedraggled tramp who made his way to the bar and began drinking heavily. When security guards tried to remove the uninvited guest from the premises, the tramp removed a putty nose, false eyebrows and whiskers to reveal none other than the Great Profile, John Barrymore.

It was into this fun-filled atmosphere that Pola Negri

made her stunning entrance. Cued as to how Valentino would be costumed, Pola wore a gown from her role as Empress of Russia in *Forbidden Paradise*. Rudolph's reaction was predictable. He asked his hostess to do the honors and Marion did. The Eagle clicked his heels, bowed and kissed the hand of the Empress.

Vilma joined the two. Their conversation sounded incomprehensible. Actually, it was nearly all English, though hardly the King's. Rudy's Italian accent was the most easily understood; Pola's Polish dialect required concentration; as for Vilma's thick Hungarian, it was anyone's guess.

"We're the Foreign Legion," Pola joked. "The others must think that we're taking over the movies."

Time would tinge Pola's remark with irony. A year later, Warner Brothers gambled on the new Vitaphone technique and added a musical background to *Don Juan*. And, in 1927, *The Jazz Singer* included a few spoken words. A new era of talking pictures was just over the horizon. When it came it would spell the end of the top foreign stars of the day. Only Greta Garbo would survive.

On November 9, 1925, *The Eagle* premiered at the Strand theater in New York. The first night audience was wildly enthusiastic. Spotlights followed Rudolph Valentino to the stage as the audience rose to its feet applauding and cheering. Visibly moved, the actor thanked all his fans for their loyalty to him. Giving credit to all who worked on the film, he bowed three times and made his exit.

Critics compared his athletic feats to those of Douglas Fairbanks; his horsemanship to that of Tom Mix; and called his acting the finest ever. For Rudolph, it was a joyous but incomplete moment. Natacha was not with him to share his vindication.

She arrived in New York aboard the *Leviathan*, returning from Europe on November 10 in time to read the reviews. At dockside she greeted the reporters, poised and confident. No, she said, she had not spoken with her husband nor did she intend to call him. Any conversation between them would have to be at his instigation. She was happy to learn that *The Eagle* had been received so well and hoped that the movie in which she would be making her debut as an actress would be as well received. Its title was a significant epitome: *When Love Grows Cold.*

If Rudolph had any thoughts of contacting Natacha before he left for England to make a personal appearance at the premiere of *The Eagle,* he may have been dissuaded by a call he received from a gentleman who referred to himself as Benjamin Conner. Conner notified Valentino that he had just returned from Paris with Natacha. While there, he had filed suit for divorce in her behalf.

When the *Leviathan* made its return voyage to Europe, Rudolph Valentino was among those on board. He was traveling alone.

UNCHARTED SEAS

In London, he was again greeted with acclaim. Crowds had lined up during early afternoon for the premiere that evening and the streets in front of the Marble Arch Pavilion were soon choked by a mob of several thousand people, only a few hundred of whom could possibly get in. Fifteen British pounds, over sixty dollars, was offered for tickets and turned down. As Valentino entered the roped-off walkway that led to the entrance, the crowd pushed forward in near hysteria. The actor was protected by a cordon of English bobbies, as women leaped forward in an attempt to touch him.

British critics were warm in their praise for *The Eagle*. Valentino caught the boat train for Paris where he contacted attorneys to represent him in Natacha's divorce action. He enjoyed the nightlife of gay Paree with the Dolly sisters, Jean Nash, and newly-divorced Mae Murray.

New Year's Eve found Rudolph in Monaco. A few days later, asked if he was planning to marry again soon, he answered, "On New Year's night, just as midnight ushered in 1926, I made a vow never to marry again, and I backed my pledge by accepting a five-to-one bet of ten thousand dollars that I will still be unmarried in 1930. The bet is registered at the sporting club at Monte Carlo and I am already counting the ten thousand dollars as my own."

From Monaco, Rudolph went to Juan les Pins for a tender, agonizing reunion with the couple who had become his surrogate parents. They embraced emotionally, their faces wet with tears.

Rudolph met with his family—Maria, Alberto, Ada and Jean—on his return to London. After several relaxing days of sightseeing and shopping, he kissed Maria goodbye and boarded a ship for America with Alberto and his family.

In California, they detrained in Pasadena to avoid the hassle of reporters at Union Station in Los Angeles.

The next few weeks were to be good ones. Rudolph was a magnanimous host, and he took Alberto and his family on sightseeing tours around Southern California and shopping at the finest stores in town. There were parties at Pola's mansion in Beverly Hills.

There was also a housewarming at Falcon's Lair attended by everybody who was anybody in the movie colony. Valentino lived extravagantly. His latest European purchases had added to his growing collection of medieval and Renaissance art and artifacts. In addition, he had brought back costly gifts for all of his friends, including a monogrammed black onyx cigarette case, studded with diamonds, with a matching cigarette holder for Pola.

Ullman was forced to call Rudolph aside to inform him that his finances had been depleted. Pola probed into his despondency and learned of his financial condition. At her insistence, he borrowed fifteen thousand dollars, promising to pay it back as soon as he could. Then, he met with Schenck and—after signing a new contract for $200,000 per picture plus 25 percent of the profits—he agreed to star in *The Son of the Sheik,* a sequel to the film that had rocketed him to superstardom. This was surprising and undoubtedly a result of his financial needs since he had grown to hate constant identification as "The Sheik."

The sequel would concern twin sons born to the marriage of Sheik Ahmed Ben Hassad and Lady Diana Mayo. The initial plan was to have Rudolph play both of the twins, using the newly-developed split-screen technique for scenes showing the twins together. But it was decided to combine the roles of the twins. Instead, Rudolph would play both the father and the son.

Meantime, Rudy and Pola enjoyed the Saturnalian revels of a movie colony riding the crest of opulence.

Many gatherings were held at the homes of neighbors in Beverly Hills. The most elegant were at Pickfair, the home of Douglas Fairbanks and Mary Pickford. At one memorable dinner for three hundred given by Gloria Swanson, guests found either a solid gold compact or cigarette case beside their place settings.

Along the shores of the Pacific in Santa Monica, exclusive affairs were hosted by Irving Thalberg and Norma Shearer at their austere French provincial home. Further down the beach, the lavish parties thrown by Marion Davies at her ninety-room Georgian villa were breathtaking in scope. Guests dined in one of three dining rooms or in the enormous banquet hall. They watched movies in the baronial library, imported from a chateau in Europe, where, at the touch of a button, a section of the floor would rise to form a screen. They played tennis on one of several courts. They swam in one of two pools—the larger of which measured eighty feet in length. At one party, Marion had a circus carousel installed on the grounds. Always in attendance was the prodigious William Randolph Hearst.

For sheer size, Marion's parties would be dwarfed only by those of her paramour at his castle in San Simeon. These were usually weekend affairs. Guests arrived either by plane—using the private landing strip on the grounds—or on a special train met by limousines that would whisk them off to the imported and restored castle with its satellite of three villas atop a mountain overlooking the Pacific. There was never a lack of something to do. The four hundred thousand acres surrounding the castle were equipped with facilities for every type of recreation and included one of the best stocked zoos in the Western Hemisphere.

The inevitable call came, however, and Valentino went to work on *The Son of the Sheik*. Location for much of the desert scenes were the dunes outside of Yuma, Arizona. Here the director assembled a cast that included Agnes Ayers, recreating her role of Lady Diana, and Vilma Banky as Yasmin, the love of the young Sheik.

It was a gruelling ordeal that all in the company would never forget. Spring that year was unusually hot on the Arizona desert—both day and night. The company found it virtually impossible to get adequate rest before their four a.m. call. Sand got into everything. Grit was everpresent in the food. Desert flies—large, fearless and voracious—swarmed everywhere. Vilma Banky was horrified when she reached for what she believed to be a bowl of blackberry jam and found that it was a sugar bowl alive with flies. Montague Love, playing the archvillain Gabah the Moor, got deathly ill from drinking brackish water. When the company finally moved to Los Angeles to finish the movie within the confines of the United Artists lot, Valentino was noticeably thinner and appeared physically drained.

As spring moved into the summer, Rudolph spent his days quietly. He would saddle his favorite gray gelding, Ramadan, while Pola was at Paramount beginning her work on *Hotel Imperial,* and ride the hills alone, with only Kabar, the Doberman, for company. On Sundays he and Pola went down to the harbor where the *Phoenix,* a gift from Natacha, was docked, and sailed down the California coast. The hot sun and the fresh spray seemed to ease the tension that lay deep within him.

They attended the wedding of Mae Murray to Prince David Mdivani. Photographers shot him tight-lipped and drawn, the unmerciful sun highlighting the bags that had begun to settle under his eyes. "Five more years," he remarked, noting that his hair was thinning and the lines were becoming ingrained in his face. "That's about all I have left as a star. By then I should have enough money to be independent. Then I'll go into something else. I can produce. I can become a director."

His dream was to work six months a year, making two films. The other six months he wanted to spend along the Riviera in France.

They attended a party given by Joe Schenck and Norma Talmadge at the beach house owned by Norma's sister, Constance. It was in honor of Richard Barthlemess on his birthday. Fatty Arbuckle—who kept solvent by an occasional directing job under the facetious pseudonym, Will B. Good, was there, as well as Lolly Parsons, Mae Murray with her Prince, Ronald Colman, Bessie Love, Carmel Myers, Bea Lillie, Blanche Sweet, Jack Pickford, Agnes Ayers and Michael Reachie. Here Rudolph met a shy, reserved young man who had just joined the Hollywood community and was interested in how movies were made— a tall, darkly handsome man named Howard Hughes.

The Son of the Sheik was given a special invitational preview in Burbank. When the film ended, his fellow members of the Hollywood community along with journalists and exhibitors rose as one to give him a standing ovation. Later, Pola recalled, "The film was not one of his best but the animal magnetism missing in his last few performances had returned with all its former power. The audience stood and cheered. I wept for joy."

Leaving the theater they ran into the usual crowd of autograph hunters and celebrity seekers. While he and Pola were signing autographs he caught a glimpse of a short, stoutish woman who had just left the theater.

"Junie," he shouted. He pushed his way through the crowd to embrace June Mathis. It had been a long time since they had last spoken, and as June gave way to the unrestrained joy in his embrace, she felt the old anger within herself dissipate.

The public premiere of *The Son of the Sheik* was held at Grauman's Million Dollar theater in downtown Los Angeles. Rudolph and Pola attended in the company of Charles Chaplin, Louella Parsons, Mae Murray and Prince Mdivani. Again the audience was wildly enthusiastic and he was called on stage to say a few words. He had just completed a short speech when he noticed that some of the more eager members of the audience had edged up the stairs at both ends of the stage. Those to his left inadvertently put their weight against a fourteen-foot-high urn. As it toppled toward the occupants of the front-row seats, Valentino jumped across the stage and tried to steady it, but the weight was too great. He deflected its fall, however, but he and the urn fell into the orchestra pit. Rudolph was knocked unconscious. It was some time before the doctors could bring him around.

Although bruised from the fall, Valentino pronounced himself completely fit and refused medical attention. He proceeded to concern himself with last minute preparations for the personal appearance tour of *The Son of the Sheik*. Alberto and his family were about to return to Europe and he bade them good-bye, promising to meet them in New York prior to their sailing. He then caught a train for San Francisco.

In the city by the bay, he was the guest of Mayor James R. Rolph at a luncheon at the Fairmont Hotel where, broke and hungry nine years before, he had met with Norman Kerry and asked about the motion picture business. Rolph, a dog fancier, was a good friend of the movie actor and only the year before had made him a present of one of his dogs.

Three nights later he was in Chicago with the Ullmans for an overnight stay before catching the New York Special. The midwestern city in mid-July was sweltering under an intense heat wave that had gripped much of the nation. From his suite on the top floor of the Blackstone Hotel, Rudolph stood by the open windows and looked out past the sweep of Grant Park to where the murky gray of Lake Michigan merged with leaden skies.

He had once found these trips exciting. Viewing strange new cities from the windows of his hotel suite, he would feel compelled to get out into the streets to taste the exhilaration that each one offered. Now, looking out from his windows, he sensed nothing but emptiness.

A pounding on the door interrupted his thoughts. He opened it to an agitated George Ullman.

"Rudy, have you read the *Tribune?*"

Before he had a chance to answer, Ullman shoved the paper at him. It was opened to the editorial page and Ullman pointed his finger to an article entitled "Pink Powder Puffs." The writer had visited a new public ballroom in Chicago. Visiting the men's washroom he found: "a contraption of glass tubes and levers and a slot for the insertion of a coin. The glass tubes contain a fluffy, pink solid, and beneath them one reads an amazing legend which runs something like this: 'Insert coin. Hold personal puff beneath the tube. Then pull the lever.'

"A powder-vending machine: In a men's washroom? *Homo Americanus!* Why didn't someone quietly drown Rudolpho Guglielmi, alias Valentino, years ago?

"And was the pink powder vending machine pulled from the wall or ignored? It was not. It was used. We personally saw two *men* step up, insert coin, hold kerchief beneath the spout, pull the lever, then take the pretty pink stuff, and put it on their cheeks in front of the mirror."

The article concluded: "It is a strange social phenomenon and one that is running its course not only in America but in Europe as well. Chicago may have its powder puffs; London has its dancing men and Paris its gigolos. Down with Decatur; up with Elinor Glyn. Hollywood is the national school of masculinity. Rudy, the beautiful gardener's boy, is the prototype of the American Male.

"Hell's bells. Oh, Sugar."

Rudolph's first reaction was to take a cab to the *Tribune* and confront the writer. Ullman had to argue with him, telling him that would be ridiculous. "There must be a hundred or more writers there, Rudy. How are you going to find the one who wrote the article? He didn't have the guts to sign it, did he? Do you think that he's going to step forth and admit he did it? Hell, no! You'll just end up making yourself a laughing-stock. And if you start anything, they'll call the cops—and it's their town. You know, with Big Bill Thompson as mayor, who's going to win out, don't you?"

Rudy paced the floor, slamming his fists into the wall. Tears of fury filled his eyes.

"Not only did he insult me, he insulted my name! He insulted my father and my father's father!"

Eventually, it was decided that Rudolph would challenge the writer to a duel—not with guns, or foils, but in a boxing ring. The challenge was printed in the *Chicago Herald-Examiner*.

To the Man (?) Who Wrote The Editorial Headed "Pink Powder Puffs":

The above-mentioned editorial is at least the second scurrilous personal attack you have made upon me, my race, and my father's name.

You slur my Italian ancestry; you cast ridicule upon my Italian name; you cast doubt upon my manhood.

I call you, in return, a contemptible coward, and to prove which of us is the better man, I challenge you to a personal test. This is not a duel in the generally accepted sense—that would be illegal. But in Illinois, boxing is legal, so is wrestling. I therefore, defy you to meet me in the boxing or wrestling arena to prove in typically American fashion (for I am an American citizen), which of us is more of a man ...

I will meet you immediately or give you reasonable time in which to prepare, for I assume that your muscles must be flabby and weak, judging by your cowardly mentality ...

I want to make it plain that I have no grievance against the *Chicago Tribune* although it seems a mistake to let a cowardly writer use its valuable columns as this "man" does. My fight is personal—with the poison-pen writer of editorials that stoops to racial and personal prejudices ... I welcome criticisms of my work as an actor—but I resent with every muscle in my body, attacks upon my manhood and my ancestry.

Hoping I will have an opportunity to demonstrate to you that the wrist under a slave bracelet may snap a real fist into your sagging jaw, and that I may teach you respect of a man even though he may prefer to keep his face clean, I remain with

Utter Contempt,
Rudolph Valentino

In a postscript he added that he would be returning to Chicago in ten days and that an answer to the challenge be sent to him in care of United Artists in New York.

The challenge went unanswered. On the train to New York, Ullman caught Valentino drinking a glass of bicarbonate of soda.

"Still bothering you, huh?"

Valentino grimaced and nodded. "Maybe you're

right about my seeing a doctor, George. Make an appointment for me when we get in New York, okay?"

The stomach pains Rudy had been suffering had gotten worse. Ullman made an appointment with Dr. Harold G. Meeker and Valentino went to see him. According to Dr. Meeker, nothing seemed to be seriously wrong with the actor. "Keep away from all that rich food you've been eating and cut out some of those spicy Italian dishes," he advised. "Get a lot of rest and see me in another week."

Rest was not easily scheduled. On July 24, Rudolph saw Alberto and his family off at the dock. The following afternoon he was at the Mark Strand theater for the first showing of *The Son of the Sheik*. Again he was mobbed and the buttons were ripped from his jacket.

The following day he accepted a challenge from Frank "Buck" O'Neill, boxing reporter for the *New York Evening Journal*. O'Neill, in behalf of the journalistic fraternity, wanted to find out whether or not the man who had issued a challenge to the Chicago writer could actually fight. At six-foot-one and weighing over two hundred pounds, O'Neill was taller and much heavier than Valentino. However, it soon became apparent that O'Neill had spent more time at his typewriter and in bars than he had in a gym—he was considerably out of shape. Nevertheless, he managed to land a good left hook to Valentino's head and brought tears to the actor's eyes with a solid right to the nose. Rudolph, however, landed the best punch of the fight —a right hook aimed at the jaw that O'Neill, in ducking, caught on the side of his head. It sent him reeling and he fell on the hard gravel roof of the hotel where the fight was staged.

Minutes later, the writer, stunned and out of breath, called it quits, suggesting a round of drinks. "That guy has a punch like a mule. I wouldn't like to have him sore at me."

Two days later, Rudolph returned to Chicago as promised. Learning that his adversary had still not come out of hiding he issued a statement in the *Herald-Examiner* that began, "It is evident you cannot make a coward fight any more than you can draw blood out of a turnip . . ." Claiming vindication, he made a personal appearance at the opening of *The Son of the Sheik* at the Roosevelt Theater and returned to New York, feeling much better. Two days later he made another personal appearance at Atlantic City.

Returning from New Jersey, he accepted an invitation from Gus Edwards to see his revue at the Ritz-Carlton Hotel. Afterwards, Edwards introduced Valentino and asked the actor to join him onstage where he presented him with a pair of boxing gloves. After lengthy applause, Edwards said, "I think the folks would like to see you dance, Rudy. I know I would."

The orchestra struck up a tango. Valentino, choosing a partner from the revue, moved gracefully into the provocative steps of the dance that had brought him acclaim in *The Four Horsemen*. It would be his last tango before an audience.

On August 6, he joined his old friend Jack Dempsey and his actress-wife, Estelle Taylor, at the premiere of *Don Juan* at the Warners' Theater on Broadway. In the title role was John Barrymore and Estelle was Lucrezia Borgia. Mary Astor played a virgin who eventually won Barrymore's heart. Included in the cast were Myrna Loy and, in a bit part, a young actress named Hedda Hopper.

The evening was a harbinger of things to come. A filmed introduction presented czar Will Hays: "You are witnessing," came his flat midwestern dialect from speakers placed behind the screen, "a new era in motion picture history."

Accompanying *Don Juan* were a series of short features in which classical musical artists sang arias from operas and played violin and piano selections. As for *Don Juan,* it was merely a silent film to which an orchestral background score had been added—roughly synchronized with the film. There were no spoken words; dialogue was still supplied by printed titles.

After a personal appearance at the Strand in Brooklyn, Rudy had a week to rest before his final date in Philadelphia. But rest he would not. Something was driving him. He seemed to be racing against time. He sought to mend fences, and those who could provide him with a philosophical insight into himself. And he pursued pleasures compulsively.

He sought out Jean Acker who was in Manhattan preparing for the opening of a Broadway play. They went night-clubbing, and the gossip columnists were quick to note. He was seen with Marian Benda and Elsie Janis. Then, out of the clear blue, he called Adolph Zukor, inviting him to lunch at the Colony. Valentino preferred nothing but the best.

Minutes after they had been seated, every woman in the restaurant was aware of the presence of the Great Lover. Women Zukor barely knew rushed up to say hello. Valentino apologized to Zukor for the problems he had caused and spoke of his desire to direct when his acting career was over.

He dined with H. L. Mencken, the leading essayist on American customs and mores. He sought out Adela Rogers St. John, the chic chronicler of America's social set, and charmed her.

St. John was interested in his romantic involvements. She asked about Pola and he answered that she had phoned him that she would be coming to be with him in New York soon.

Then he was off into the bathroom, rummaging about for bicarbonate of soda, explaining that he had eaten too many snails for lunch. He added, grinning, "Pola always drives me to bicarbonate of soda."

St. John made a perceptive stab, "You're still in love with Natacha, aren't you."

The answer came with little hesitation. "I will always be in love with Natacha. She is the only woman I have ever loved, ever will love. In the courts she divorces me. Can you divorce in the heart?"

A few minutes later he waved from the doorway and was gone.

August 13, 1926, was fraught with significances. It fell on a Friday, and it was also the anniversary of the day that Natacha left Rudolph in Los Angeles with prints of *What Price Beauty?*, the trip that marked the end of their relationship. Rudolph spent that Friday the 13th with Joseph Schenck and his wife Norma Talmadge. Again he complained of stomach pains, which seemed to have increased in severity and centered at the lower right of his abdomen. Schenck, considerably concerned, asked Rudy if his appendix had been removed. Receiving a negative reply, he suggested, "Promise me you'll call a doctor, first thing tomorrow."

The following evening Valentino dropped by the suite occupied by George Ullman and his wife, indicating that he was on his way out to have dinner with some friends. Ullman noticed that Valentino looked pale and drawn, and asked him how he felt.

"I'm fine, George. The old stomach has been bothering me but I'm all right now."

Ullman suggested that Valentino make it a short evening.

Early the following morning, Ullman was awakened by a phone call. It was Barclay Warburton, Jr., a New York broker and friend of Rudolph's. "Can you come over right away?" Warburton asked in a voice tight with strain. "Rudy's very sick and I think we'd better call a doctor."

Ullman rushed to Warburton's apartment. He found the actor in great pain. He called Dr. Meeker who then called Dr. Paul Durham. Shortly after noon, the Polyclinic Hospital received a request for an ambulance to be sent to Dr. Durham.

At six p.m. that evening—Sunday, August 15— Dr. Meeker, assisted by Drs. Durham and Battey, the latter senior house physician for the hospital, removed a ruptured appendix and stitched up a hole in Valentino's stomach. The attending doctors then met with Dr. George Manning, who had been called in for consultation, and released a report that the actor had suffered from "an acute gastric ulcer and a ruptured appendix and, as in cases of this kind, peritonitis had sent in." However, they believed that "the effects of peritonitis had been checked . . . the crisis would be expected within the next forty-eight hours."

Valentino's condition was given as "grave."

He was placed in a private suite in the hospital— the same one Mary Pickford had occupied fourteen years before. There were two rooms and a private bath and soon the anteroom was filled with flowers, fruit and candy. Valentino requested that they be given to other patients in the hospital.

The world received the news in black newspaper headlines: **VALENTINO COLLAPSES.**

Bulletins on his condition became a daily story on the front pages of all newspapers.

Dateline: August 17—"Tomorrow to bring crisis in Rudolph Valentino's fight for his life against the ravages of peritonitis. Death watch established. At 7 p.m.: temperature 103.6; respiration 26; pulse 106."

A cable arrived from Douglas Fairbanks and Mary Pickford, vacationing in Paris: "VERY SORRY TO HEAR OF YOUR SUDDEN ILLNESS. BUT WE KNOW YOUR MARVELOUS CONSTITUTION WILL AID RECOVERY."

The telephone switchboard was jammed with phone calls from all over the nation. A second switchboard was ordered and installed. Mayor Jimmy Walker telephoned, as did Mae Marsh and Jean Acker. Pola Negri called from the Coast. She would catch a train on Sunday. The studio would not permit her to travel by air.

A wire arrived from Charles Chaplin: "KEEP UP THE GOOD FIGHT BECAUSE EVERYBODY NEEDS YOU."

The next day, the news seemed promising.

Dateline: August 18: "Valentino on mend. Condition of star improving. Patient still gravely ill but definite progress towards recovery reported. Telephone operators flooded with inquiries while mail and wires pour in."

A cryptic cable arrived from Natacha in France: "GOOD WISHES." Valentino was noticeably cheered when the message was read to him. Among the hundreds of telegrams that arrived, two were from his former leading ladies, Vilma Banky and Bebe Daniels.

John Gilbert, whose roles were modeled after Valentino's, wired: "FIGHT, FIGHT, FIGHT. MILLIONS NEED YOU."

At 6 a.m. a call came in from Los Angeles. "This is Pola Negri. How is Mr. Valentino?" The operator answered that there was no change in his condition.

The news became increasingly positive.

Dateline: August 19: "Valentino winning. Sheik of screen past crisis. Actor voices thanks from bed to well-wishers who remembered him. Drs. Durham, Meeker, Manning state that they will issue no further reports."

Dateline: August 21: "Valentino continues to improve. Screen star gaining in strength already thinks of place to convalesce."

A wire arrived from Pola: "WILL BE COMING IN ABOUT A WEEK."

Then, a sudden reversal took place.

Dateline: Sunday, August 22: "Valentino's condition reported very serious. Blood transfer likely. Pleurisy in left chest."

The doctors refused to become alarmed. At 1:10 p.m. they issued the following report: "There is a slight spread of the infection in the abdominal wall causing considerable discomfort. Nothing to cause undue anxiety at this time. Temperature 101; respiration 22; pulse 90."

By evening, the situation seemed much more critical: "Temperature 103.2; respiration 26; pulse 120."

In his hospital suite, Valentino was in pain and his breathing was labored. He said to Joe Schenck who was at his bedside, "I didn't know I was so near death on Sunday. I am beginning to realize only now how serious my condition was."

Schenck assured him that he would soon be well and recuperating in Maine where the fishing was good. Valentino looked over at Dr. Meeker. "Bring your own gear, Doc. All my extra tackle's in L.A."

Outside Polyclinic Hospital, dusk had darkened the city. People from all over began gathering in front of the hospital, drawn by curiosity, love, and the scent of impending disaster.

PART THREE

"What the average man calls Death. I believe to be merely the beginning of Life itself. We simply live beyond the shell. We emerge from out of its narrow confines like a chrysalis. Why call it Death? Or, if we give it the name Death, why surround it with dark fears and sick imaginings?

"I am not afraid of the Unknown."

—Rudolph Valentino
(from his diary)

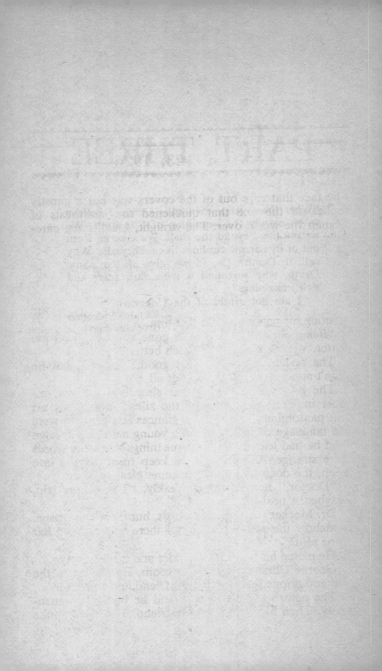

The face that rose out of the covers was but a ghostly replica of the one that quickened the heartbeats of women the world over. The straight, black hair, carefully slicked back on the screen, was rumpled, the cheeks gaunt, the lips unusually red, the eyes bright with fever. The ordeal of the emergency operation and the complications that had followed had taken their toll.

"*Comé sta,* Rudy?" the doctor asked, using the greeting his patient had taught him.

"*Bene, dottore.* The pain is gone now. Surely, I am better. Very weak still but much better."

The doctor nodded. "Very good," he said, but he didn't mean it. It wasn't good at all.

The patient's breathing was slow and shallow, almost imperceptible. Star of the silent screen, his art was pantomime. Expressions, glances and gestures were the language of his craft. As a young man in a foreign land he had learned to sense meanings when the words were strange. As he fought to keep from drifting into sleep, the doctor's attitude became clear to him.

"Doctor," he called out weakly. "The fishing trip. Maybe the next time we meet."

Dr. Meeker searched for words, but there were none. Somehow the patient knew and there was nothing left to be said.

He patted his patient's shoulder and turned away.

George Ullman entered the room. He moved to the bed and gripped the hand of his friend and employer.

The actor's eyelids opened and he blinked momentarily. Then he recognized his friend. His voice spoke strained and low. "Wasn't it an awful thing that we were lost in the woods last night?"

Ullman nodded. He was bewildered.

"Don't you get it, George? That was a joke."

"Yes, Rudy, I know. But you had me going for a minute."

Ullman gripped the actor's hand. Tears filled his eyes. Abruptly, he turned away. The skies beyond the windows were beginning to lighten. He went to the window and began to lower the shades.

The whisper from the bed was strained. "No, George. Leave them up. I want the sunlight to greet me."

Ullman gained control of himself. Returning to the bedside he spoke of the millions who were praying for Valentino. He said he had cabled Natacha. He said it would be all right soon. And then he had run out of things to say and he told his friend that he should rest, that he would be back.

Outside, in the wide corridor guarded by security men, he saw Joseph Schenck and broke down. "I just couldn't stay there and watch him die, Joe."

Schenck went in to see the young man. "Keep fighting," he told Valentino. "The fish are waiting for you in Maine."

"Don't worry, Chief. I'll be all right."

A short while later the patient lapsed into semi-consciousness. Occasionally, he stirred and called out in Italian. Daylight bathed the room but the sun that the actor loved so much was shrouded in heavy clouds and the light was weak. By eight a.m. he was comatose, drifting into deep sleep. At ten he was partially awakened so that he might hear the last rites performed by Father Joseph M. Congedo of the Church of the Sacred Heart of Jesus and Mary. It was said that Father Congedo was from Castellaneta and had known the actor as a child.

Shortly before eleven, Jean Acker arrived. She was the last visitor admitted to the room. The patient was not conscious when she leaned over and kissed him, tears streaming down her face.

At 12:10 p.m., Rudolph Valentino was pronounced dead.

BEYOND THE ROCKS

The news went out quickly to a waiting world.

From a hospital room commandeered by newsmen the words went by phone to city desks. Typewriters clattered; linotypes clanked; and the words were cast into lead stereotypes clamped to cylinders of giant rotary presses. Ink pressed into paper. Paper folded, trimmed, tied into bundles; tossed from trucks onto street corners where the word would again be audible in the shouts of newsboys racing down the streets: "Extra! Extra! Read all about it! Rudolph Valentino Dead!"

One-fifth of the nation's homes had radios. To others, this was the way the news came.

In front of the hospital, the crowd estimated at nearly a thousand at the time of the actor's death had almost doubled. By 1 p.m., West 50th Street between Eighth and Ninth Avenues had become a solid mass of humanity. Calls for ambulances and police reinforcements continued through the night.

Ullman cabled Alberto in Paris, Maria in Rome and Natacha in Juan les Pins. Schenck, concerned about the size of the mob outside of the hospital, called Campbell's Funeral Church, suggesting that the body be removed from the hospital as quickly as possible, using a private exit at the side of the building.

Flags at all Hollywood studios were lowered to half-mast. United Artists and Paramount closed their doors in mourning.

Pola Negri had slept late. She was awakened by the ringing of the phone. It was a reporter calling from New York.

Rudy had often used a ruse when answering the phone—claiming to be his valet. Pola pretended to be her maid.

"How is Miss Negri taking the news of Valentino's death?" the reporter asked.

Half-awake, she had to ask the caller to repeat the question. Comprehension and shock arrived simultaneously.

In Juan les Pins, Natacha had used a more unusual means of communication. The previous Friday, a cable had arrived from Ullman: "RUDY IS IMPROVING. WELL ON THE WAY TO RECOVERY." That evening, in an optimistic mood, she held a seance with George Wehner, an American medium. Jenny, Black Feather and Meselope had "come through from the other side." Both Jenny and Black Feather indicated that they would stay with Rudy during these hours of crises. Then the Egyptian spirit, Meselope, took over with a recitation of Rudolph's life, career and character. This was followed by an announcement that Rudy's time on earth was nearing an end and, in a few days, he would be passing "to another plane of consciousness of this ever-continuing life."

Disturbed by Meselope's statements, Natacha cabled Ullman the following morning. She had not received a reply when she awoke Monday morning to the heavy scent of tuberoses in her bedroom—a scent that had never been in her room before. It was then that she realized her ex-husband was dead.

European newspapers were filled with stories of Valentino's death. Millions the world over joined the millions of Americans in mourning. Seldom in the history of the world had the death of a single individual evoked so great an emotional response.

Pola Negri, distraught, asked to be taken to Falcon's Lair. There in the rambling white house with its taupe interior walls, she walked from room to room, reliving memories and calling out the name of her love. It was an hour before she could be taken away.

The New York dawn of Tuesday, August 24, was sullen and gray. By eight a.m., a crowd had begun to assemble in front of Campbell's Funeral Church on

Broadway at 66th street. According to George Ullman, Valentino had requested that the public be allowed to view his remains. Campbell's would open its doors at six p.m. for this purpose.

The crowd rapidly increased in size. Campbell's decided to move up its opening time to four p.m. The Campbell's staff was hard at work preparing the body for viewing. The work that had to be done to the face was extensive, since the poison that ravaged the body had grossly distorted the features. The artificial look that resulted gave rise to rumors that a wax replica of the star had been substituted.

A little after noon, a gentle rain began to fall. The temperature was in the high 80's. The crowd was then estimated to number twelve thousand and it was still growing. Most of those massed together were somber, but there were scattered elements of a carnival atmosphere. Sidewalk vendors moved about selling hot dogs, lemon ice, cold drinks and newspapers.

As the crowd grew it became increasingly unruly. A decision was made to open earlier than planned. When attendants moved towards the doors, the crowd surged forward and the plate glass windows in front gave way. Much of the glass fell outward toward the street. Three policemen, who had been trying to hold the crowd back, were pushed through the windows and badly cut. Two were hospitalized with sprained backs. Among many others injured, the majority were women in their early twenties.

Mounted policemen and hundreds of policemen on foot charged into the mob, waving nightsticks to push back the screaming, hysterical people. The doors of the funeral parlor were closed until order could be restored. Those who entered in the first surge seemed more intent on gathering souvenirs than viewing the body that lay carefully spotlighted on a catafalque in the majestic Gold Room of the funeral church. A later assessment of the damages revealed that a huge potted palm had been knocked over, many of its fronds stripped away. Floral displays had been ravaged and chairs had been overturned. The room might have been struck by a tidal wave.

Ullman was angry. "This crowd will do anything. They'll rip buttons off of his coat and some will try to touch his face," he said. The body was removed from the catafalque, placed in a silver and bronze casket, and taken into a smaller room upstairs that had an emergency exit leading out to 66th Street. Here a new setting was arranged with large bunches of red roses, a crucifix and a statue of the Virgin Mary placed behind the open coffin. Lighted candles were placed at the head and foot.

An emergency first-aid station was set up in a separate room within the funeral church. A "Dr. Sterling Wyman" presented himself and immediately took charge of the operation, directing special nurses hired for the emergency.

By four p.m. the police had miraculously managed to create a semblance of order. They had pushed, jostled and menaced the crowd into a line, four abreast, that circumambulated six city blocks, but moved, more or less, in an orderly manner. The doors were again opened and everything went smoothly until a little after six p.m. when those who had finished their day's work at offices and factories began to arrive. Many newcomers could see little reason for waiting in line. They went straight to the front of the funeral church, and were held in check there by a line of police. As this crowd increased in size, belligerent and jeering, a call for assistance brought fifty more policemen and Police Commissioner McLaughlin himself who ordered that the new group be driven back. Chaos took place when the crowd, tempers worn thin by the heat of the long day, charged the police.

By eight p.m. when dusk began to settle over the city, the police had once again gained control. Broadway, in front of Campbell's, gave evidence of the many battles that had been waged. The wet, glistening asphalt was littered with debris—shoes, hats, torn clothing, broken umbrellas and shattered bottles.

When the doors were closed at midnight over fifty thousand people had passed by the bier and another ten thousand were still standing in the streets. It was decided to continue the public viewing from nine a.m. to midnight for the next two days.

In the opinion of Acting Captain Hammill, a twenty-year veteran of the New York police department who had spent years in crowd control at the Polo Grounds, the crowd of that day had been without equal for sheer size and unruliness.

Shortly after the doors had been closed, ten men dressed in black shirts appeared. They identified themselves as members of the Fascisti League of America. They said they had received cabled instructions to place a wreath on the bier and stand guard over the coffin at night. After a consultation with Ullman, funeral officials granted permission.

The next day was a slightly more orderly version of the first. Again the crowd assembled well before the doors were to be opened. This time the police were waiting for them. All went well, with only minor disturbances, until the midnight hour arrived and the police cut off the line, permitting only the two hundred closest to the entrance to enter. The several thousand people remaining charged the police and again rioting ensued.

Ullman decided that he had had enough. He called off the public viewing scheduled for the third day stating, "From now on the body will only be viewed by friends and associates under my personal supervision. The lack of reverence shown by the crowd, the disorder and attendant rioting have forced me to this decision."

There were other reasons for Ullman's decision. The employees of Campbell's and the police had been under a severe strain. Over one hundred and fifty thousand people had passed by the bier and the crowd was still to wane. Further, the appearance and the courtesies extended to the Fascist guards had resulted in repercussions from many quarters.

Jean Acker, accompanied by her mother and a cousin, had come to pay her respects the second day. She managed to maintain her composure as she walked slowly around the coffin, her eyes on the lifeless face.

But just as she was leaving, she broke into tears and had to be supported into another room. When she had pulled herself together sufficiently, she granted a brief interview to the press.

"We had always retained our love for each other. My affection for him has always been of a motherly or sisterly nature," she said. Then, recalling that she was the last visitor to see him alive, she went on to say, "All I remember is that white face on the bed and his labored breathing. I wanted to do something to help him but it was all so hopeless. I had never seen anyone dying before. When he died, I was in an adjoining room."

Life had relegated Jean Acker to secondary roles in the shadow of giants like Nazimova and Valentino. Now, for a moment she found herself on center stage, caught in the glow of the public spotlight. But, her moment of glory was brief. The next star was just outside the wings. Pola Negri's private Pullman car had just arrived in Chicago and was being coupled to the Twentieth Century Limited for the final leg of its cross-country journey.

Pola's entrance, staged before a large crowd that had gathered at New York's Grand Central Station, was pure theater. She was met in her private car by Mr. and Mrs. Ullman and Dr. Sterling Wyman, a member of the group since his mysterious appearance at the emergency first-aid station at Campbell's. Ullman and Wyman helped Pola from the train. As they entered the station proper, Pola saw the huge waiting crowd. Emitting a loud scream, she fainted. Revived, she continued to scream as she was helped to a waiting limousine and taken to the Ambassador Hotel. Inside the lobby of the hotel that had been Valentino's last home, she fainted again.

In due course, she reached Campbell's. Kneeling beside the coffin, Pola again collapsed.

The site chosen for the New York funeral of Rudolph Valentino on August 30 was both appropriate and ironic. It was St. Malachy's, called the Actor's Church, located on West 49th between Broadway and Eighth Avenue. Thirteen years before, a young immigrant had come down this exact street—alone and apprehensive—searching the house numbers through narrowed eyes. He had stopped a few doors away from St. Malachy's at an apartment house known as Giolitto's. In death he had been brought back to a street where almost one hundred thousand now thronged. Among his pallbearers was the mayor of the city. His life in America had taken him full cycle but he would not know the full measure of his triumphs.

Simultaneously, services were held in other cities. In Chicago, two thousand gathered at the Trianon Ballroom on the south side. In Los Angeles, Firefly, the horse that Valentino had ridden in *Son of the Sheik,* was saddled and, with inverted boots in its stirrups, walked by Norman Kerry, Emmett Flynn and George Fitzmaurice at a special memorial in his honor. Coinciding with the services in New York, work at all motion picture studios and locations was halted for two minutes of silent tribute.

Alberto Guglielmi arrived in New York two days later aboard the *Homeric.* He was met at the pier by Pola, the Ullmans and Dr. Wyman, who had assumed the position as Pola's private physician. Alberto was escorted to Campbell's where he visited the body of his brother alone.

Afterwards, Alberto met with reporters. With tears in his eyes, he made a statement that endeared him to Valentino's American fans, "My brother belongs to America and he will be buried in California, which he loved." He went on to say that plans were underway for an impressive shrine to house his brother's body. Until this memorial was constructed, it had been decided to accept an offer from June Mathis to use a family crypt at the Cathedral Mausoleum in the Hollywood Memorial Park Cemetery.

On September 2, the casket was placed on one of two special cars provided by the railroads. An entourage that included Alberto, Pola, the Ullmans, Frank Campbell, Harry Klemfuss and W. H. Hull—the latter two, respectively, the press agent and the manager of Campbell's Funeral Church—boarded the second car for the long ride to the West Coast.

On September 7, final services for the man who had become known the world over as the Great Lover were held at the Church of the Good Shepherd in Beverly Hills. Thousands lined the route of the funeral procession as it left the church and moved along Santa Monica Boulevard, past the studios of United Artists, to the cemetery that butted up against the buildings that marked the back lot of Paramount. Overhead, along the route of the processional, a small plane hired by Luther Mahoney, Valentino's faithful employee, sprinkled the streets with roses.

In a crypt loaned by June Mathis, Rudolph Valentino was laid to rest.

And the legend of Rudolph Valentino was born.

THE SONS OF THE SHEIK

In the days of mourning that followed, reports of suicides by women came from all over the world. The most publicized of these was Peggy Scott, a twenty-eight-year-old British actress who swallowed poison. Notes she left behind suggested that she had met the actor in Biarritz "in 1922, and Rudolph helped me carry on. He told me a lot of his own sufferings. I have had lots of wonderful moments. There's a lot I cannot tell . . ." In New York, Mrs. Angelina Celestina shot herself while clasping a picture of Valentino to her bosom. Other Valentino-related suicides were reported in Japan and Italy.

Lyricists J. Keirn Brennan and Irving Mills joined with composer Jimmy McHugh to turn out a song entitled "There's a New Star in Heaven Tonight." It found immediate popularity but it lacked the staying power of Smith-Wheeler-Snyder's "The Sheik of Araby."

A short time after the burial, it was learned that the black-shirted Fascist guards who had been sent "on the orders of Benito Mussolini" had actually been hired by Campbell press agent Harry Klemfuss for publicity purposes.

Dr. Sterling Wyman, it was discovered, was an imposter. While he had claimed to be "Pola Negri's personal physician," "the house physician for Campbell's Funeral Church," and "an old friend of George Ullman," he not only did not have a medical degree, but the closest involvement he had had with any institution whatsoever had been the times he had spent locked up in: The State Hospital for the Criminally Insane at

Dannemora; the Federal Penitentiary at Atlanta; the Elmira Reformatory.

Two genuine doctors who had constantly been at Valentino's side were feeling the effects of the long siege. Dr. Harold Meeker had to abandon practice for several days while he recovered from exhaustion. Dr. Paul Durham was in a much more critical situation, having suffered a heart attack. He was placed under hospital care.

Another enigmatic figure also sought the sanctity of a sanatorium. He was Barclay Warburton, Jr., who disappeared into the Harbor Sanatorium at 667 Madison Avenue immediately after Valentino was hospitalized. According to reports issued, he was undergoing an operation, the nature of which was never explained. Warburton's incapacitation combined with the suddenness of Valentino's illness and the conflicting accounts regarding his last evening led many to give credence to rumors of poisoning.

The first reports of Valentino's illness—consistent in all newspapers—indicated that he had collapsed in his apartment at the Ambassador in the presence of his valet, the only other occupant in the apartment. These reports went on to say that the valet summoned Warburton who, in turn, called Ullman. The latter called the doctors.

Reporters interviewed a Harry Richman who stated that he had been present at a party at Warburton's apartment that Saturday evening. Valentino had attended with Marian Kay Benda, a Ziegfeld Follies beauty with whom he had been seen about town. "About one-thirty," Richman said, "Rudy became violently ill and was rushed to his apartment at the Ambassador." To this extent, Richman's statement coincided with all other reports given at that time.

Warburton refused to answer questions, saying only that there had been no party. The following day he was incommunicado in the sanctity of the sanatorium.

Other stories began to appear. The *New York Daily News* ran two separate stories that touched on that evening. One concerned a request by a Dr. M. Del Vecchio for an autopsy on Valentino's body. Dr. Del

Vecchio suspected the actor had been poisoned. The story went on to say that Valentino had been the guest of honor at a party at the Warburton apartment that began at ten p.m. and ran into the wee hours in the morning. Around 8:30 a.m., all the guests had left except for Valentino and four others. It was then that the actor became ill, and Dr. Durham had been called. The doctor, upon arrival, had called for the ambulance that took Valentino to the hospital.

In the same issue, but on a different page, was an interview with Marian Benda. According to her, she and Rudy had gone out with some of his friends to several night clubs, including Texas Guinan's and the Lido. Sometime after midnight, Rudy had become ill and been taken to Warburton's apartment, at which time Dr. Durham had been called. This was all she knew since she had been taken home shortly thereafter. Barclay Warburton had been a member of the group, as had a dancer named Frances Williams. As for the others, Benda had forgotten their names.

Reporters for the *New York Graphic* turned up a cab driver named Mike Di Calzi who stated that he had picked up Valentino and Miss Benda at her apartment on West 55th street at 4:30 a.m. and driven them to the Warburton address on Park Avenue. "Mr. Valentino looked to be in the best of health at that time," Di Calzi is quoted as saying. The cab driver's story was corroborated by a Frank Gross who operated the elevator in Marian Benda's building.

The *Graphic* also published a statement made by the ambulance driver from the Polyclinic Hospital who had answered Dr. Durham's call. He was quoted as saying, "I arrived at the Park Avenue address Sunday morning and, in the drawing room I saw a young man dressed in a flowered lounging gown writhing in pain on a divan. When Dr. Durham and I helped him to his feet he clutched at his sides and moaned with agony."

He went on to state that he had driven this young man to the hospital and Dr. Durham had followed in his car. Upon their arrival, an intern had helped him take the patient upstairs. He did not know until much later that his passenger had been Rudolph Valentino.

The motives for poisoning were given as either jealousy or revenge. Dr. Del Vecchio's request for an autopsy was based on his understanding that the facial features of the actor had "lost all semblance of characteristics in life." This was strong evidence of "poisoning by a foreign substance." According to the doctor, "Septic poisoning alone would not do that."

Contradicting these rumors was Pearl Frank, one of the three nurses who had been at the star's bedside during the days of his ordeal. Miss Frank, located at her home, told reporters, "There is absolutely nothing to the poison story."

When Alberto arrived from Paris, he was also inclined towards suspicions, "I can't understand it. He always kept himself in perfect condition. He was only thirty-one and I never knew him to have a sick day in his life."

Later, after reading Dr. Meeker's medical report—incorporated into a press release by "Dr. Sterling Wyman," at the time still regarded as an eminent authority—which gave the cause of death as a "ruptured gastric ulcer and general peritonitis," listing contributing causes as "septic pneumonia and septic endocarditis," Alberto placed his faith in the report and requested that there be no autopsy.

Reporters cornered Joseph Schenck to ask about Valentino's estate. Schenck replied that while he was not qualified to answer, he doubted that it would be extensive. "Rudy spent money as fast as he made it. On money matters," said Schenck, "Rudy was like a little boy."

When the terms of Valentino's will were disclosed, many were surprised. Alberto Guglielmi and Maria Guglielmi Strada had each been granted one third of the estate. The remaining third was to be given to Mrs. Teresa Werner of Salt Lake City, aunt of the deceased's former wife, Natacha. Neither Jean Acker nor Pola Negri were mentioned, but Natacha was not ignored. She had been bequeathed "the sum of one dollar, it being my intention, desire and will that she receive this sum and no more."

Mrs. Werner indicated grateful surprise. Alberto and

Maria stated that they were considering contesting the will. As for Pola, she brought action against the estate a few months later to recover the sum of $15,000 which, she stated, she had loaned to the actor after his funds had been depleted by his European trip.

When Natacha returned to the States on November 25, 1926, reporters asked her reactions to the will. Her reply was that she found no fault with it and would not contest it. She bore Rudy no malice, she said. In fact, she had been in constant communication with him. She then introduced George Wehner who had returned on the same ship. Wehner, she said, had been a guest at her parents' chateau and was a medium associated with the American Society for Psychical Research.

Asked about her conversations with her dead ex-husband, Natacha announced that Rudy had informed her that he had become a citizen of the astral plane and hoped to become a legitimate actor there. He had met Enrico Caruso and had heard him sing.

She was asked if Valentino had mentioned Pola Negri. Natacha said merely, "He has made no mention of her." Having inserted the needle, she gave it a twist by adding, "Rudy only spoke to me about significant things and subjects that mean something."

Given worldwide publicity, Natacha's conversations with her dead husband brought a horde of spiritualists and believers in the supernatural into the ever-increasing ranks of the Valentino cult. This unrelenting interest, which packed theaters featuring Valentino movies long after his death, led to a continuing search for another Valentino. Actors Edmund Carewe, Antonio Moreno, John Gilbert, Ramon Navarro and Ronald Colman were cast, with varying degrees of success, in roles patterned after those of the Great Lover. A Mexican named Luis Antonio Damaso de Alonso borrowed the surnames of John Gilbert and Ruth Roland, became Gilbert Roland. In a remake of *Camille* with Norma Talmadge in 1927, he established himself as a contender to become the new Valentino. Paramount's entry was a young man Lasky discovered at an amateur dancing contest at the Coconut Grove. Born Jack

Kranz, he had changed his name to Jack Crane. This was hardly Latin enough to suit Lasky who picked Ricardo, from his favorite brand of cigars, and added the surname of a Spanish conquistador, to bring Ricardo Cortez to the screen.

Though there were gifted actors among them, none had the sexual impact of the original. Among those to be seduced by dreams of glory was Alberto, the shorter and more staid older brother, who underwent three operations by an eminent Beverly Hills plastic surgeon, Dr. William Balsinger, in order to have a proper Valentino nose. Changing his name legally to Albert Valentino, he made his debut in *The Pride of Pleasure,* a film that offered little beyond proof that the magic of Rudolph was more than genetic. With this single ego-destroying film, the elder Valentino decided to forfeit his dreams to accept a position as an accountant with Fox, where he eventually rose to head the department.

Interest began to grow in the private life of the screen lover. Curiosities were heightened by the coincidence that his two ex-wives had been close associates of Nazimova, whose lesbian proclivities were well known within the industry. Many recalled that Jean Acker had cited a lack of cohabitation in her divorce action. Similarly, Valentino's release from bigamy charges was based on testimony that his Mexican marriage to Natacha had never been consummated. In fact, witnesses, including Doug Gerrard, had stated that Valentino had spent his wedding night not with Natacha, as might have been expected, but with his friend Gerrard.

This led to whispers that the Great Lover was either bisexual, homosexual or impotent.

Tragically, it appears that Valentino was trapped by his own public image. In a sense he had created his own Frankensteinian monster. A naive youth inclined to worship women—seeing within those whom he loved a "madonna-like quality"—had rocketed from the obscurity of bit parts into sudden fame and found himself competing with an aggressive, virile effigy, twice again as large as he, projected on a giant screen. Unfortunately, he had acted the lover much too well and women were driven to orgiastic fantasies. How could he possibly compete with that arrogant, macho image?

Marcello Mastroianni—who has known the fevered idolatry of feminine fans—on the occasion of his appearance in a stage musical based loosely on the life of Valentino, *Ciao, Rudy!*, provided an incisive look into the problems of those who become sex symbols. In an interview for *Playboy,* July 1965, he said:

"The success of a type like Valentino or Marilyn Monroe is inevitably dramatic, tragic, grotesque—because the lives of these people are always impoverished. Imagine the effort it must have taken Valentino to convince himself that he was really like his myth—or, even worse, *not* like his myth. I'm sure he made very little love. That makes you laugh? It makes me cry."

Ciao, Rudy! was neither the first, nor would it be the last, homage to the Great Lover. In the decade following his death, several studios planned movies based on Valentino's life. Eventually, the race narrowed down to Twentieth Century-Fox, Monogram and Edward Small, an independent producer. Among those considered to play the title role were George Raft and Anthony Quinn. Small won the contest when he discovered a convincing look-alike named Walter Craig, a twenty-nine-year-old dramatic actor. Craig, renamed Anthony Dexter, was given dancing lessons and a rather dull, contrived production called *Valentino* appeared in 1951, twenty-five years after the death of the famous actor.

It would be another quarter-century before television would provide its version. On November 23, 1975, Spelling-Goldberg's *The Legend of Valentino* appeared on ABC. It was not an "authentic" biography, but rather "an interpretation of the Valentino image." What resulted was a modern-day Pygmalion with Suzanne Pleshette, playing June Mathis, falling in love with Valentino, played by Franco Nero, who she discovers burglarizing her home. Through her guidance, the burglar becomes a star.

The suggestion that Mathis may have been in love with the man for whom she created heroic screen char-

acters is reasonable conjecture. If so, she lived with her
dreams until 1924 when she married Sylvano Balboni
whom she met during the filming of *Ben Hur* in Italy.
On July 27, 1927, attending a play at the 48th Street
Theater, only a stone's throw removed from St. Malachy's Church, she suffered a heart attack. As her weeping mother bent over her, Mathis, whose career had
begun in the theater, died in an alley outside of one.
Her body was taken to Campbell's Funeral Church
and from there to Hollywood where services were held.
A few weeks short of the first anniversary of Valentino's death, the body of June Mathis Balboni was
placed into a crypt adjoining his.

Natacha was destined for a longer, if not fuller, life.
Having met with little success in producing, directing,
writing and acting in films, she turned to the Broadway
stage where she again failed to set the world ablaze.
This took her into designing women's clothes, a stint as
a newspaper reporter and a futile attempt at a career
as a concert singer. In 1934, she married a Spanish
nobleman, Don Alvarado de Urzaiz, and lived with
him in Mallorca for several years. When the marriage
ended in divorce, she returned to New York where she
served as coeditor on four definitive books on ancient
Egypt. In August 1966, at the age of 69, she died in
Pasadena leaving an estate valued at $367,000.

After Valentino's death, Jean Acker moved back into the shadowed milieu to which she was accustomed.
She eventually worked as an extra. While her career
ended in the late Fifties, Jean Acker lives on in quiet
seclusion in the Los Angeles area.

Indestructible, irrepressible Pola Negri celebrated
her 78th birthday in 1977. Still chain-smoking and referring to herself as a "living legend," she makes her
home in San Antonio, Texas. In June 1927, she married Prince Serge Mdivani, brother of the Prince David
who had married Mae Murray. In late 1929, when the
Wall Street crash wiped away her fortune and "talkies"
washed away her career, Prince Serge drove away with
a new-found love in Pola's Rolls-Royce, never to return. While her long, eventful life has been seared by

tragedies, Pola continues undaunted. "My spirit is still young," she recently said.

Of these four women who were closest to Rudolph, none came forth to bid for mementos during the days that his possessions were placed before public auction.

On December 10, 1926, a crowd of over five hundred jammed into the courtyard of Falcon's Lair. Several hundred late arrivals were turned away. The occasion was a three-day auction of Valentino's effects, including two homes, horses, dogs, approximately two hundred 14th-century costumes, about the same number of shoes from the same period, cars, a 32-foot cabin cruiser, furniture, tapestries, and assorted artwork and artifacts were to be sold. The catalog for the auction was almost one hundred pages long.

The first item was Falcon's Lair itself. The bidding began at $50,000 and moved up slowly—five to ten thousand dollars at a time—until it peaked out at $115,000. At this point a telegraphed bid from Jules Howard, a New York jeweler, in the amount of $145,000 was read. No one tried to top it.

Six acres of unimproved property around the home was sold for $21,000 to the wife of Dr. Frank McCoy. Valentino's prized town car, the Isotta Fraschini, was sold for $7,900. The Avion Voisin brought only $2,200. Three American cars brought a total of only $2,432, the largest part of which was paid by Alberto Guglielmi for a Franklin coupe. Firefly, the magnificent black horse that Valentino had used in *The Son of the Sheik,* valued at around $3,000, was sold for $1,225. Bids on his three other full-blooded Arabian steeds were: Ramadan, $1,000; Haroun, $600; and Yaqui, $450.

Of Valentino's dogs, the Irish Wolfhound, Centaur Pendragon, went for much less than the $5,000 he had paid for it less than a year before. Kabar, the Doberman, and Prince, the German Shepherd, the two dogs closest to Valentino, had disappeared shortly after their master's death and were not auctioned. Months later, Prince, wasted away by hunger with his feet torn and bleeding, finally turned up in San Leandro, California. Having apparently searched in vain for his master, he died, they said, of a broken heart, on May 15, 1927. Kabar lived wild in the hills around Falcon's Lair until his death on January 17, 1929. The other three dogs, an Irish setter and two Italian mastiffs, were sold for a total of $118.

On the second day, the auction moved over to Whitley Heights where the house at 6776 Wedgwood Place was placed up before the block. When the bidding did not go beyond ten thousand dollars, the house was removed from sale. Years later, unoccupied, the constant target of vandals and souvenir hunters, it was sold to the city for $90,000. Giant bulldozers eventually came to demolish the house and carve into the hillside to make way for the new Hollywood Freeway.

It is Tuesday, December 14, 1926. The auction has moved to the Hall of Art Studios at 1753 North Highland Avenue. Along with the stable equipment that wasn't auctioned on the Friday preceding, other items to go before the block are Valentino's furniture, rugs, art objects, silver, glass and chinaware, arms and armor, cameras, jewelry, studio wardrobe, books and incidental personal effects including two large paintings designated as items numbered "268" and "269."

Item number 268 is a rich, handsome portrait of Valentino by Federico Beltran-Masses in the gaucho costuming that brought him fame in *The Four Horsemen*. It is the portrait that Pola Negri wanted for her bedroom, but Pola is not here. It is sold for $1,550.

Auctioneer A. H. Weil calls out, "Item number 269: An oil painting by the famous Spanish painter Federico Beltran-Masses, a member of the Royal Academy and a dear friend of the late actor. It is a full-length portrait of Rudolph Valentino dressed in the armor of a Persian war lord, a role he was planning for the screen. The work is titled, 'Dans le Faucon Noir,' and has been appraised as being worth $5,000. Ladies and gentlemen, how much am I bid for this beautiful work of art . . . ?"

The bidding begins at one hundred dollars and moves up slowly to three-fifty, where it pauses as the auctioneer calls for a higher bid. A thin woman in front, her hair streaked with gray, bids four hundred and there are no further bids. The auctioneer brings his gavel down thrice and announces, "Sold to Mrs. Teresa Werner for four hundred dollars . . ."

The sound of the gavel echoes over the years. It is September 16, 1976, a half-century later. The place is Arthur B. Goode Auction Gallery at 541 North La Cienega Boulevard. It is night, a little after nine p.m., and the crowd numbers approximately a hundred and fifty dressed in the casual fashion of Hollywood. At this auction, another of Valentino's portraits will go up before the gavel. This portrait, measuring thirty by forty inches and encased in an elaborate gold frame, is exquisitely done in pastel colors, predominantly pink and powder blue. The subject is undeniably Rudolph Valentino, costumed and bewigged as Monsieur Beaucaire. He had posed for the painting in the Paris studio of Gaston Albert Lavriller during his last visit to Europe, but had not lived to see the completed work. Lavriller had brought the portrait with him when he visited Hollywood in 1928. It had been purchased by a Hollywood cameraman, Ivan Dujan, who claimed to have known and worked with Valentino and described the actor as a "nice Italian guy." Now, fifty years after the death of the actor, Dujan has decided to sell his painting. It has been appraised at $5,000.

The bidding begins at $1,000 and moves up rapidly in multiples of five hundred until it reaches $4,000, where it comes to a halt. The auctioneer asks for $4,500, and receives no response. He asks for $4,250, and is still greeted with silence. Before closing out the bidding, he pitches again, "This is really a fine specimen of pastel work. It's really worth the money. Pastel is not an easy medium to paint. Can I have, uh, $4,100?"

In the front row, to the left of the auctioneer, an olive-skinned young man in his mid-thirties raises his hand, "Yes," he says. Among a Thursday-night-West-Hollywood-celebrity-curious crowd dressed in T-shirts, sloppy sweaters and jeans, he is strictly sore-thumbsville. He is too sharply dressed. Immaculate. Brown sports jacket over dark brown trousers, tan shirt and dark brown tie. He is also darkly handsome. In a Valentino look-alike contest he could be a first runner-up.

The auctioneer nods and smiles. "I have $4,100. Do I hear $4,200?" He does not. The portrait has been sold to man who gives his name only as, "Cash." There is scattered applause.

Television cameramen have been recording the auction. The newscasters ask "Cash" for interviews as the auction continues. "Cash" is involved in raising money for a film to be called *The Russ Columbo Story*. The movie will open with a scene at Valentino's funeral and the portrait will be placed next to the casket. Russ Columbo will be singing. "Cash" states that he has no sentimental attachment toward the portrait. He will put it back on auction after the film is made.

Enigmatic, obviously desiring no further publicity, he breaks off the interview and excuses himself. He walks toward the front of the building to claim his purchase. At the cashier's booth, he pulls out a sizable wad of greenbacks.

The auction continues but for the greater part of the audience the night's drama has ended. They move with shuffling steps toward the exit where the brisk Southern California night awaits.

Along the sidewalk a television crew is loading heavy cases into a large panel truck that bears the letters "CBS-TV." Tonight, newscaster Nathan Roberts will give a special report on the Eleven O'Clock News about a man who has been dead for fifty years.

It will not be the last report on a screen lover whose legend is eternal.

FILMOGRAPHY
(In order of production, release dates as indicated)

*1914 MY OFFICIAL WIFE Vitagraph
Director: James Young
Cast: Clara Kimball Young, Earle Williams, Harry T. Morey

*1916–17 PATRIA Wharton, Inc.-International Film Service
Directors: Leopold & Theodore Wharton, Eastern episodes;
           Jacques Jaccard, Hollywood episodes
Cast: Irene Castle, Milton Sills, Warner Oland, Dorothy
      Green, George Majeroni, Nigel Barrie
A fifteen-episode serial. Valentino is said to have appeared in
the third episode.

1918 ALIMONY First National
Director: Emmett J. Flynn
Screenwriter: Hayden Talbot
Cast: Josephine Whittel, Lois Wilson, Ida Lewis, George
      Fisher, Alice Taffe (Terry)

1918 THE MARRIED VIRGIN Fidelity
Director: Joseph Maxwell
Screenwriter: Hayden Talbot
Cast: Vera Sisson, Kathleen Kirkham, Edward Johnson, Frank
      Newberg, Lillian Leighton
Not released until 1920. In 1922, at the height of Valentino's
popularity, it was re-released as FRIVOLOUS WIVES.

1918 THE DELICIOUS LITTLE DEVIL Universal
Director: Robert Z. Leonard
Screenwriter: Harvey Thew, adapted from a story by Harvey
              Thew and John Clymer
Cast: Mae Murray, Harry Rattenbury, Richard Cummings,
      Ivor McFadden, Bertram Grassby, Edward Johnson

---

*Credited by some film historians. Participation considered dubious
since Valentino—in recounting his early years in New York—never mentioned appearances in these films, nor have others who were close to
the actor.

1918 THE BIG LITTLE PERSON Universal
Director: Robert Z. Leonard
Cast: Mae Murray, Allen Sears, Clarissa Selavigny

1918 A SOCIETY SENSATION Universal
Director: Paul Powell
Screenwriter: Douglas E. Doty, adapted from a story by Perley
                Poore Sheehan
Cast: Carmel Myers, Alfred Allen, Fred Kelsey, Harold Good-
        win, Zazu Pitts
Valentino received billing in this film as: M. Rudolphe de
Valentina.

1918 ALL NIGHT Universal
Director: Paul Powell
Screenwriter: Fred Nyton, adapted from a story, "One Bright
                Idea," by Edgar Franklin Stearns
Cast: Carmel Myers, Charles Dorlan, Mary Warren, William
        Dyer, Wadsworth Harris, Jack Hall, Lydia Yeamans
        Titus

1919 A ROGUE'S ROMANCE Vitagraph
Director: James Young
Screenwriter: James Young, adapted from a story by H. H.
                Van Loan
Cast: Earle Williams, Brinsley Shaw, Herbert Standing, Kath-
        erine Adams, Maude George

1919 THE HOMEBREAKER Ince-Paramount
Director: Victor Schertzinger
Production supervised by: Thomas Ince
Screenwriter: R. Cecil Smith, adapted from a story by John
                Lynch
Cast: Dorothy Dalton, Douglas MacLean, Edwin Stevens,
        Frank Leigh, Beverly Travers, Nora Johnson, Mollie
        O'Connell

1919 VIRTUOUS SINNERS Pioneer
Director: Emmett J. Flynn
Cast: Norman Kerry, Wanda Hawley, Harry Holden, Bert
        Woodruff

1919 OUT OF LUCK Griffith-Artcraft-Paramount
Director: Elmer Clifton
Production supervised by: D. W. Griffith
Cast: Dorothy Gish, Ralph Graves, Raymond Canon, George
        Fawcett, Emily Chichester, Porter Strong, Kate V.
        Toncray

1919   EYES OF YOUTH   Equity
Director: Albert Parker
Screenwriter: Albert Parker
Cast: Clara Kimball Young, Milton Sills, Edmund Lowe,
      Pauline Starke, Gareth Hughes, Sam Southern, Ralph
      Lewis

1920   AN ADVENTURESS   Republic Distributing Co.
Director: Fred J. Balshofer
Screenwriter: Fred J. Balshofer, adapted from a story by
              Charles Taylor and Tom J. Geraghty
Cast: Julian Eltinge, Virginia Rappe, Leo White
Re-released in 1922—after Valentino's rise to fame and Vir-
ginia Rappe's notoriety in the Arbuckle case—as THE ISLE OF
LOVE.

1920   THE CHEATER   Metro Pictures
Director: Henry Otto
Screenwriter: Lois Zellner, based upon the play "Judah" by
              Henry Arthur Jones
Cast: May Allison, King Baggott, Frank Currier, Harry Van
      Metter, May Giracci, Percy Challenger, Lucille Ward

1920   PASSION'S PLAYGROUND   First National
Director: J. A. Barry
Screenwriter: Adapted from a story by C. N. and M. A.
              Williamson
Cast: Katherine MacDonald, Norman Kerry, Nell Craig, Ed-
      win Stevens, Alice Wilson, Howard Gaye, Virginia
      Ainsworth

1920   ONCE TO EVERY WOMAN   Universal
Director: Allen J. Hollubar
Cast: Dorothy Phillips, Margaret Mann, William Ellingford,
      Elinor Field, Emily Chichester, Robert Anderson
Also released as AMBITION.

1920   STOLEN MOMENTS   Pioneer
Director: James Vincent
Screenwriter: Richard Hall, adapted from a story by H.
              Thompson Rich
Cast: Marguerite Namara
Also released as THE WONDERFUL LOVE.

1920   THE WONDERFUL CHANCE   Selznick
Director: George Archainbaud
Screenwriters: Mary Murillo and Melville Hammett, adapted
               from a story by H. H. Van Loan
Cast: Eugene O'Brien, Martha Mansfield, Tom Blake, Joe
      Flanigan, Warren Cook

1921 THE FOUR HORSEMEN OF THE APOCALYPSE   Metro Pictures
Director: Rex Ingram
Screenwriter: June Mathis, adapted from a novel by Vicente
            Blasco Ibañez
Cast: Alice Terry, Pommeroy Cannon, Josef Swickard, Brins-
      ley Shaw, Alan Hale, Mabel Van Buren, Stuart Homes,
      Jean Hersholt, Bridgetta Clark, Nigel De Brulier, Wal-
      lace Berry, John Sainpolis, Bull Montana, Mlle. Dolorez,
      Beatrice Dominguez, Bodwitch "Smoke" Turner, Minne-
      haha, Ramon Novarro

1921 UNCHARTED SEAS   Metro Pictures
Director: Wesley Ruggles
Screenwriter: George Elwood Jenks, adapted from a story by
            John Fleming Wilson
Cast: Alice Lake, Fred Turner, Carl Gerard, Rhea Haines,
      Charles Hill Mailes

1921 CAMILLE   Metro Pictures
Director: Ray C. Smallwood
Producer: Alla Nazimova
Screenwriter: June Mathis, adapted from the novel and play
            "La Dame Aux Camelias" by Alexandre Dumas
Art Director: Natacha Rambova
Cast: Alla Nazimova, Arthur Hoyt, Zeffie Tilbury, Rex Cherry-
      man, Patsy Ruth Miller, Edward Connelly, Consuelo
      Flowerton, William Orlamand

1921 THE CONQUERING POWER   Metro Pictures
Director: Rex Ingram
Screenwriter: June Mathis, adapted from the book "Eugenie
            Grandet" by Honore de Balzac
Cast: Alice Terry, Ralph Lewis, Edna DeMary, Edward Con-
      nelly, George Atkinson, Mary Hearn, Willard Lee Hall,
      Ward Wing, Mark Fenton, Ramon Novarro, Bridgetta
      Clark
Also released as EUGENIE GRANDET.

1921 THE SHEIK   Paramount
Director: George Melford
Screenwriter: Monte M. Katterjohn, adapted from a novel by
            Edith M. Hull
Cast: Agnes Ayres, Walter Long, Adolph Menjou, George
      Waggner, Lucien Littlefield, Patsy Ruth Miller, F. R.
      Buttler

1922 MORAN OF THE LADY LETTY   Paramount
Director: George Melford

Screenwriter: Monte M. Katterjohn, adapted from a novel by
Frank Norris
Cast: Dorothy Dalton, Charles Brigley, Emil Jergensen, Maude
Wayne, Walter Long, George Kuwa, George O'Brien,
William Boyd

1922 BEYOND THE ROCKS Paramount
Director: Sam Wood
Screenwriter: Jack Cunningham, adapted from a story by Eli-
nor Glyn
Cast: Gloria Swanson, June Elvidge, Alec B. Francis, Edith
Chapman, Gertrude Astor, Helen Dunbar, Mabel Van
Buren

1922 BLOOD AND SAND Paramount
Director: Fred Niblo
Screenwriter: June Mathis, adapted from a novel by Vicente
Blasco Ibañez
Cast: Lila Lee, Nita Naldi, Rose Rosanova, George Field,
Gilbert Clayton, Fred Becker, Leo White, Dorcas Ma-
thews, Walter Long, Charles Belcher, Jack Winn, Wil-
liam E. Lawrence, Sidney De Gray, George Periolat

1922 THE YOUNG RAJAH Paramount
Director: Philip Rosen
Screenwriter: June Mathis, adapted from the play "Amos
Judd" by Alethea Luce and a novel by John
Ames Mitchell
Cast: Wanda Hawley, Charles Ogle, Fanny Midgely, Bertram
Grassby, J. Farrell MacDonald, Pat Moore, Josef Swick-
ard, Maude Wayne, Edward Johnson, Robert Ober,
George Periolat, William Boyd, Spottiswoode Aitken

1924 MONSIEUR BEAUCAIRE Paramount
Director: Sidney Olcott
Screenwriter: Forrest Halsey, adapted from the novel by Booth
Tarkington and the play by Evelyn Greenleaf
Sutherland
Cast: Bebe Daniels, Lowell Sherman, Lois Wilson, Paulette
Duval, Doris Kenyon, John Davidson, Oswald Yorke,
Flora Finch, Lewis Waller, Ian MacLaren, Frank Shan-
non, Brian Donlevy

1924 A SAINTED DEVIL Paramount
Director: Joseph Henabery
Screenwriter: Forrest Halsey, adapted from the novel "Rope's
End" by Rex Beach

Cast: Nita Naldi, Helena D'Algy, Dagmar Godowsky, Antonio D'Algy, Claire West, George Siegmann, Louise La Grange, Jean Del Val, Robert Lytton, Frank Montgomery

1925 COBRA Ritz-Carlton Pictures-Paramount
Director: Joseph Henabery
Screenwriter: Anthony Coldewey, adapted from a novel by Martin Brown
Cast: Nita Naldi, Casson Ferguson, Gertrude Olmstead, Claire de Lorez, Eileen Percy, Hector V. Sarno, Lillian Langdon, Henry Barrows, Rose Rosanova

1925 THE EAGLE Astor Pictures-United Artists
Director: Clarence Brown
Screenwriter: Hans Kraly, adapted from the novel "Dubrovsky" by Alexander Pushkin
Cast: Vilma Banky, Albert Conti, Louise Dresser, James Marcus, George Nichols, Mack Swain, Carrie Clark Ward, Gary Cooper

1926 THE SON OF THE SHEIK United Artists
Director: George Fitzmaurice
Screenwriters: Frances Marion and Fred De Gressac, adapted from the novel "The Sons of the Sheik" by Edith M. Hull
Cast: Vilma Banky, Agnes Ayres, George Fawcett, Montagu Love, Karl Dane, Bull Montana, William Donovan, Erwin Connelly, Charles Requa, Bynunsky Hyman

BIBLIOGRAPHY

The American Heritage History of the Twenties & Thirties, Editors of the American Heritage, Editor in Charge, Ralph K. Andrist. American Heritage Publishing Co., subsidiary of McGraw-Hill, 1970.

Anger, Kenneth. *Hollywood Babylon.* Dell Publishing, 1975.

Ardmore, Jane. *The Self-Enchanted.* McGraw-Hill, 1959.

Arnold, Alan. *Valentino.* Hutchinson & Co., 1952.

Ben-Allah (Newman), *Rudolph Valentino.* Ben-Allah Co., 1926.

Blum, Daniel. *A Pictorial History of the Silent Screen.* Grosset & Dunlap, 1953.

Brownlow, Kevin. *The Parade's Gone By . . .* Alfred A. Knopf, Inc. 1968.

Carter, Randolph. *The World of Flo Ziegfeld.* Praeger Publishers, 1974.

Chaplin, Charles. My Autobiography. Simon & Schuster, 1964.

Churchill, Allen. *Remember When?* Ridge Press/Golden Press, Inc. 1967.

Dos Passos, John. *The Big Money.* Houghton Mifflin Co., 1930.

Gish, Lillian with Pinchot, Ann. *The Movies, Mr. Griffith and Me.* Prentice-Hall, Inc., 1969.

Godowsky, Dagmar. *First Person Plural.* The Viking Press, 1958.

Goodman, Ezra. *The Fifty-Year Decline and Fall of Hollywood.* Simon and Schuster, 1961.

Graham, Sheilah. *The Garden of Allah.* Crown Publishers Inc., 1970.

Griffith, Richard and Mayer, Arthur. *The Movies.* Bonanza Books, 1957.

Guiles, Fred Lawrence. *Marion Davies, a Biography.* McGraw-Hill, 1972.

Halliwell, Leslie. *The Filmgoers Companion.* Hill and Wang, 1965–1974

Hampton, Benjamin B. *History of the American Film Industry from its Beginnings to 1931.* Dover Publications, Inc., 1970.

Higham, Charles. *Cecil B. DeMille.* Dell Publishing, 1973. Originally published by Charles Scribner's Sons.

I Remember Distinctly, assembled by Agnes Rogers with comments by Frederick Lewis Allen. Harper & Brothers, 1947.

Lasky, Jesse L. with Weldon, Don. *I Blow My Own Horn.* Doubleday & Co., 1957.

Lasky, Jesse L. Jr. *Whatever Happened to Hollywood?* Funk & Wagnall, 1957.

Livingstone, Beulah. *Remember Valentino.* 1938.

MacKenzie, Norman A. *The Magic of Rudolph Valentino.* Foreword by S. George Ullman. The Research Publishing Co., 1974.

MacGowan, Kenneth. *Behind the Screen.* Dell Publishing Co., 1965 (from Delacorte Press).

Mencken, Henry Louis. *The Vintage Mencken.* Gathered by Alistair Cook, with Introduction by Cooke. Vintage Books, Inc., 1917–1955; from Prejudices, Sixth Series, Alfred A. Knopf, Inc. 1927.

Mercer, Jane. *Great Lovers of the Movies.* Crescent Books/ Hamlyn Publishers, 1975.

Morris, Lloyd. *Not So Long Ago.* Random House, 1949.

Negri, Pola. *Memoirs of a Star.* Doubleday & Co., 1970.

Oberfirst, Robert. *Valentino—The Man and the Myth.* The Citadel Press, 1962.

Palmer, Edwin O. *History of Hollywood, Volume I.* Arthur H. Cawston, 1937.

Pascall, Jeremy and Jeavons, Clyde. *A Pictorial History of Sex in the Movies.* Hamlyn Publishing Group, 1975.

Peterson, Roger C. *Valentino the Unforgotten.* Wetzel Publishing Co., 1937.

Photoplay Treasury, edited by Barbara Gelman. Crown Publishers Inc./McFadden-Bartell Corp., 1972.

Pratt, George C. *Spellbound in Darkness.* New York Graphic Society Ltd., 1973. First published by University of Rochester, 1966.

Rambova, Natacha. *Rudolph Valentino (Recollections).* Jacobsen-Hodgkinson Corp., 1927.

Robinson, David. *Hollywood in the Twenties.* Volume #3 International Film Guide Series, Paperback Library, 1968. Original edition A. S. Barnes & Co.

Rogers St. Johns, Adela. *The Honeycomb.* New American Library, Inc. 1970. Originally published by Doubleday & Company, Inc., 1969.

Rosen, Marjorie. *Popcorn Venus.* Coward, McCann & Geoghegan, 1973.

Russell, Lynn. *Voice of Valentino.* Regency Press, 1965.

Sann, Paul. *Fads, Follies and Delusions of the American People.* Bonanza Books, 1967.

Sann, Paul. *The Lawless Decade.* Crown Publishers Inc., 1957.

Scagnetti, Jack. *The Intimate Life of Rudolph Valentino.* Jonathan David Publishers Inc., 1975.

Schickel, Richard. *The Stars*. The Dial Press, 1962.

Shipman, David. *The Great Movie Stars*. Crown Publishers, Inc., 1970.

Shulman, Irving. *Valentino*. Trident Press, 1967.

Steiger, Brad and Mank, Chaw. *Valentino*. MacFadden Books, 1966.

Smith, Albert E. with Koury, Phil A. *Two Reels and a Crank*. Doubleday & Company, Inc., 1952.

Tyler, Parker. *Screening the Sexes*. Holt, Rinehart and Winston, 1972.

Ullman, S. George. *Valentino—As I Knew Him*. Macy-Masius, 1926.

Valentino, Rudolph. *Intimate Journal*. William Faro, 1931.

Wagenknecht, Edward. *The Movies in the Age of Innocence*. University of Oklahoma Press, 1962.

Walker, Alexander. *Rudolph Valentino*. Stein & Day, 1976.

Walker, Alexander. *Sex in the Movies*. Penguin Books, Ltd., 1966.

Warner, Jack L. with Jennings, Dean. *My First Hundred Years In Hollywood*. Random House, 1965.

Zukor, Adolph with Kramer, Dale. *The Public is Never Wrong*. G. P. Putnam's Sons, 1953.

Various issues and editions of the following newspapers and periodicals: *New York Times, London Times, Los Angeles Times, Los Angeles Examiner, Los Angeles Mirror, Hollywood Reporter, Variety, The Film Daily, Films in Review, Photoplay, The Players, The Saturday Evening Post, Colliers, Life, Time, Playboy, Newsweek, Motion Picture Magazine, Motion Picture Classic.*

ABOUT THE AUTHOR

VINCENT TAJIRI is a professional photographer and writer who has held such positions as editor of *Art Photography* magazine, editor of *Guns* magazine and photography editor of *Playboy* (where he created a photographic staff which was to become the largest and most efficient of any monthly magazine in publishing history). Tajiri's current efforts have involved editorial directorship on four recently published photographic books, two touring photographic exhibitions, and two new book projects. He lives in southern California with his wife and two of his three children.

Bantam Book Catalog

Here's your up-to-the-minute listing of every book currently available from Bantam.

This easy-to-use catalog is divided into categories and contains over 1400 titles by your favorite authors.

So don't delay—take advantage of this special opportunity to increase your reading pleasure.

Just send us your name and address and 25¢ (to help defray postage and handling costs).